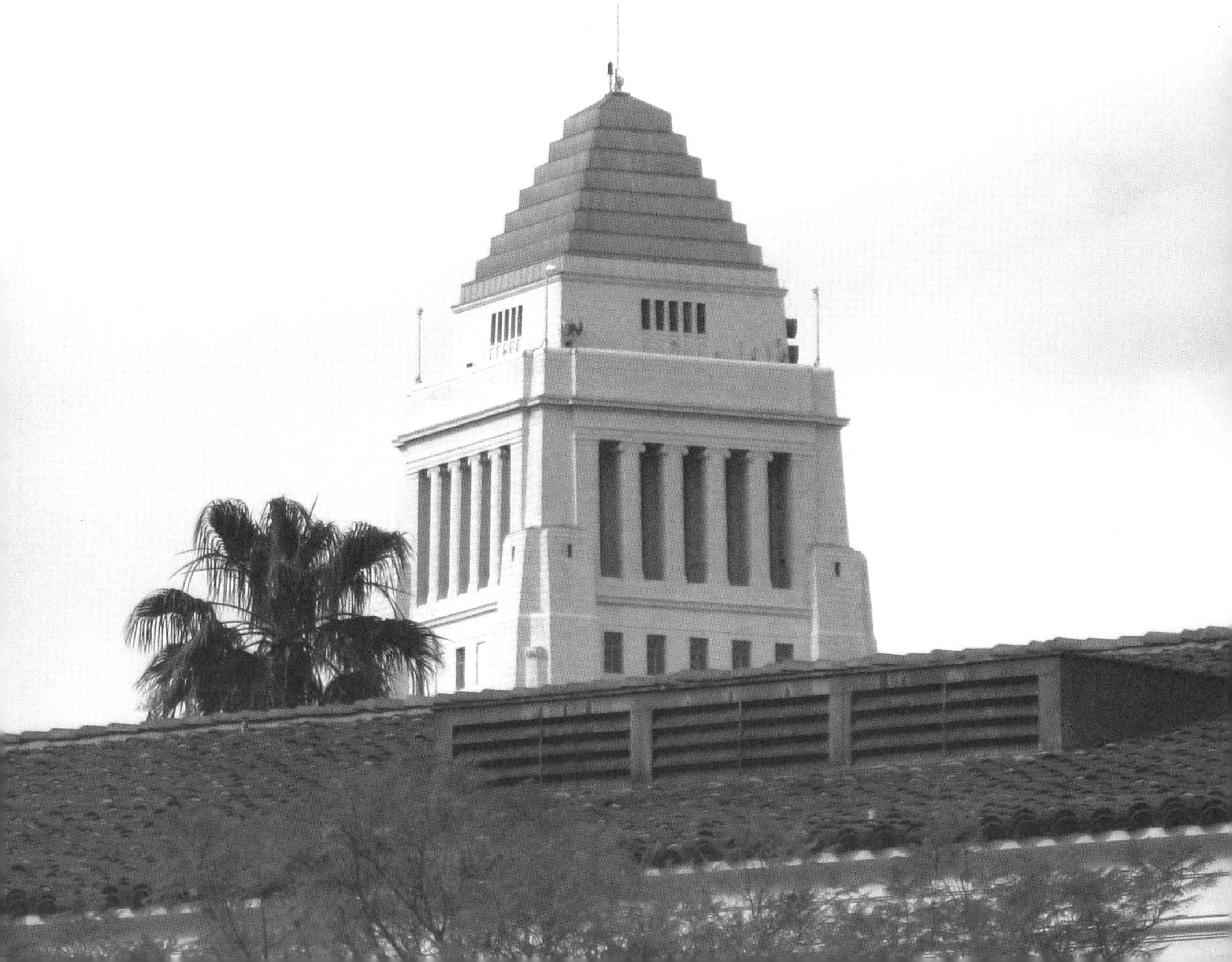

ICONIC VISION

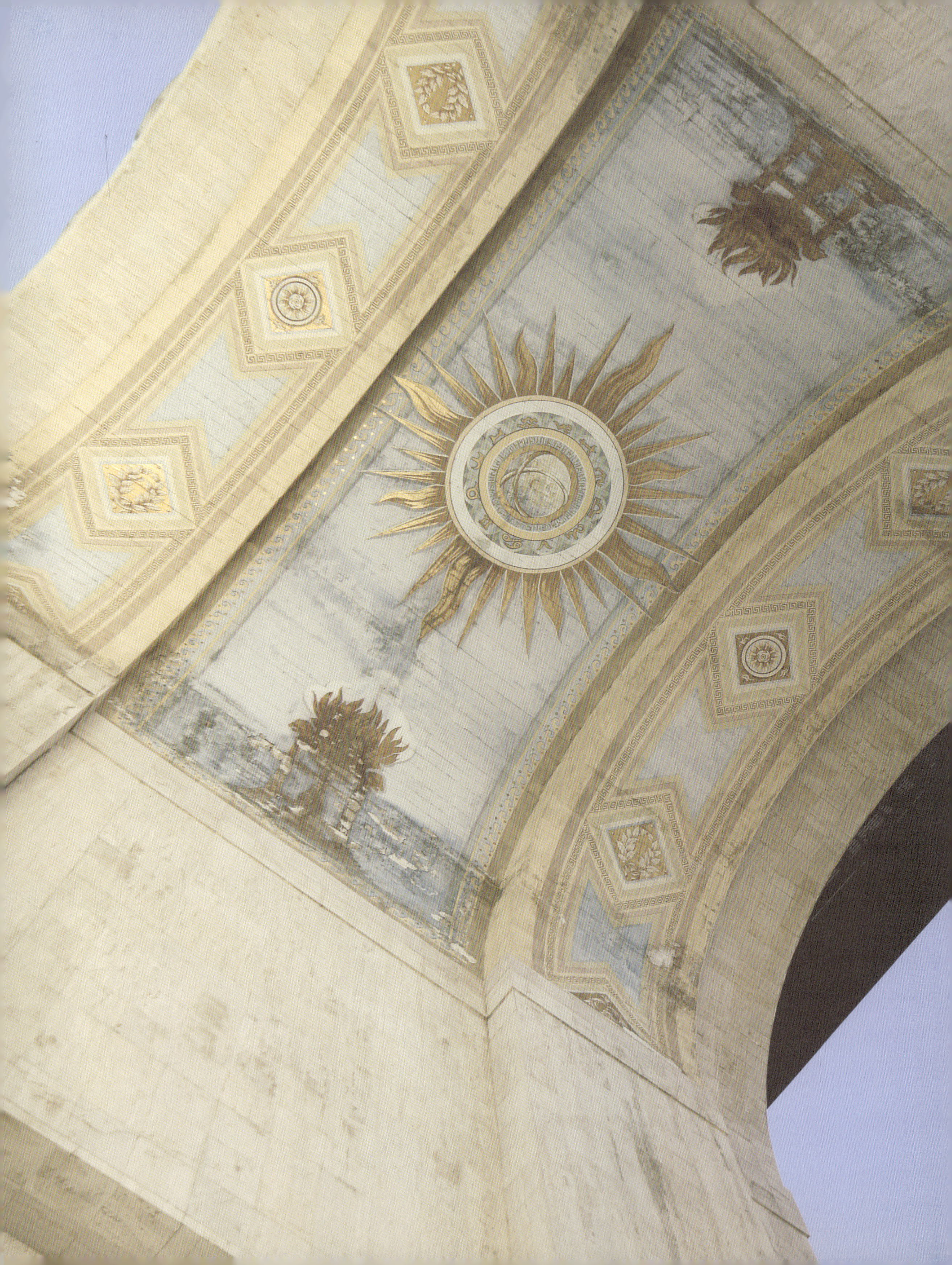

ICONIC VISION

John Parkinson
Architect of
Los Angeles

Stephen Gee

Angel City Press

JOHN PARKINSON AND
JOHN C. AUSTIN SHORTLY
AFTER THEY EACH
ARRIVED IN LOS ANGELES,
TOGETHER ON THE
MOUNT LOWE RAILWAY

to Vera and Reginald Clear

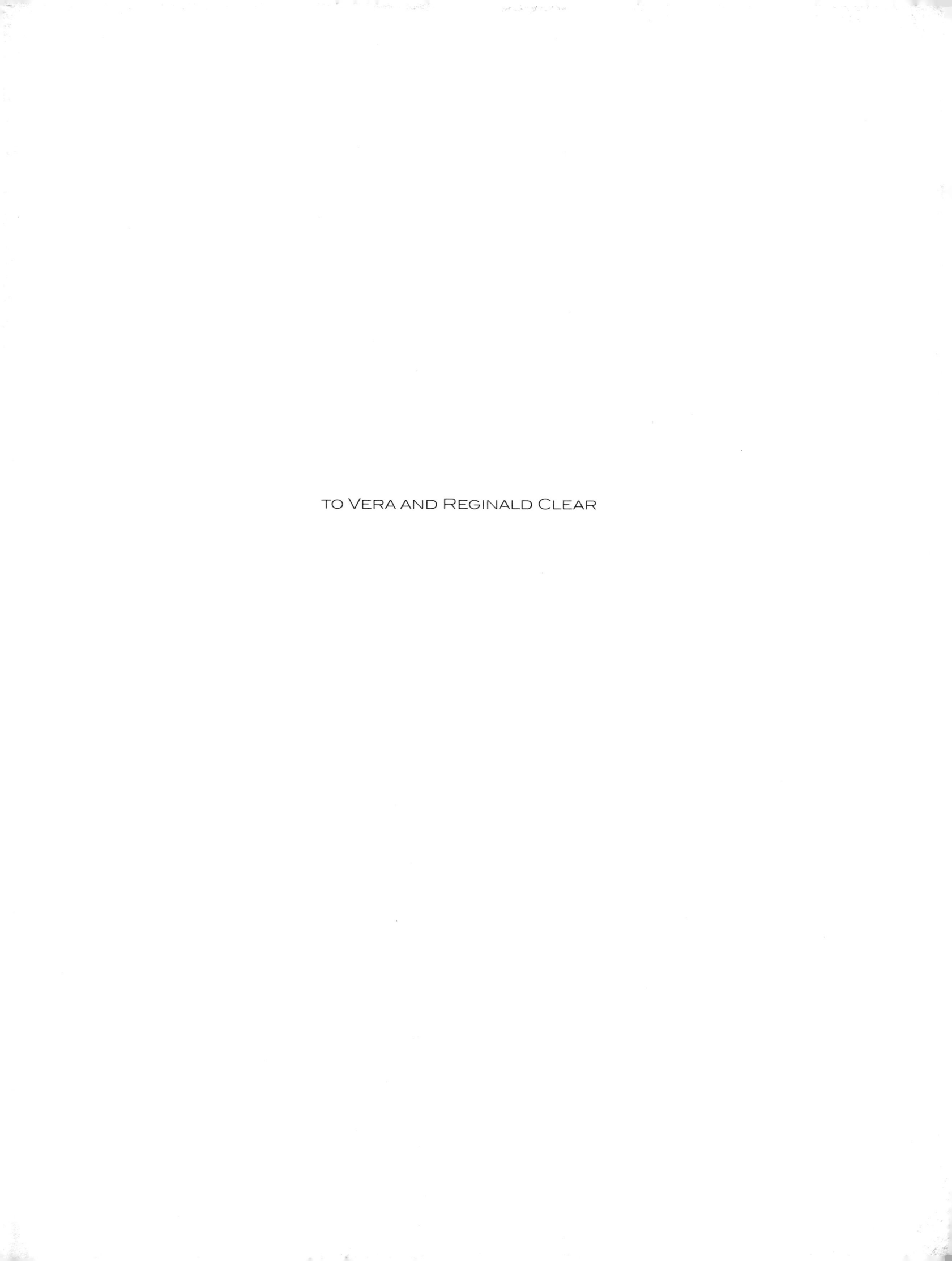

CONTENTS

Introduction 10

From the Ground Up 12

Born in England 18

Seattle 36

Los Angeles 54

Parkinson & Bergstrom 76

War, Trade and Education 96

John & Donald Parkinson 108

Parkinson Icons 126

Los Angeles Memorial Coliseum 128

City Hall 144

Bullock's Wilshire 164

Union Station 180

Acknowledgments 196
Photo Credits 198
Bibliography 200
Index 204

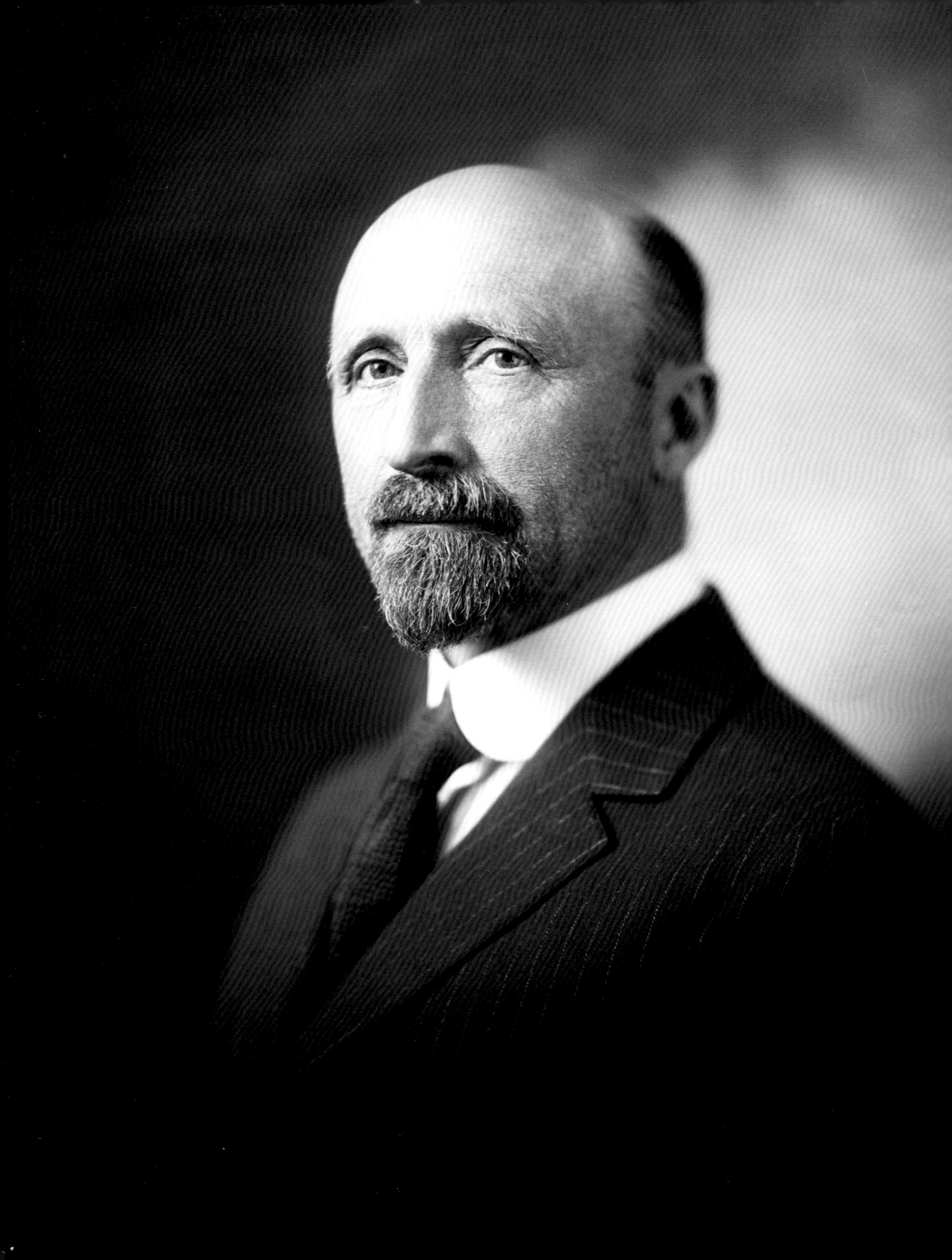

Future citizens have only to walk through the streets of Los Angeles to be reminded how much John Parkinson in his lifetime contributed to the city that grew up under his hand.

—*Los Angeles Times*, December 12, 1935

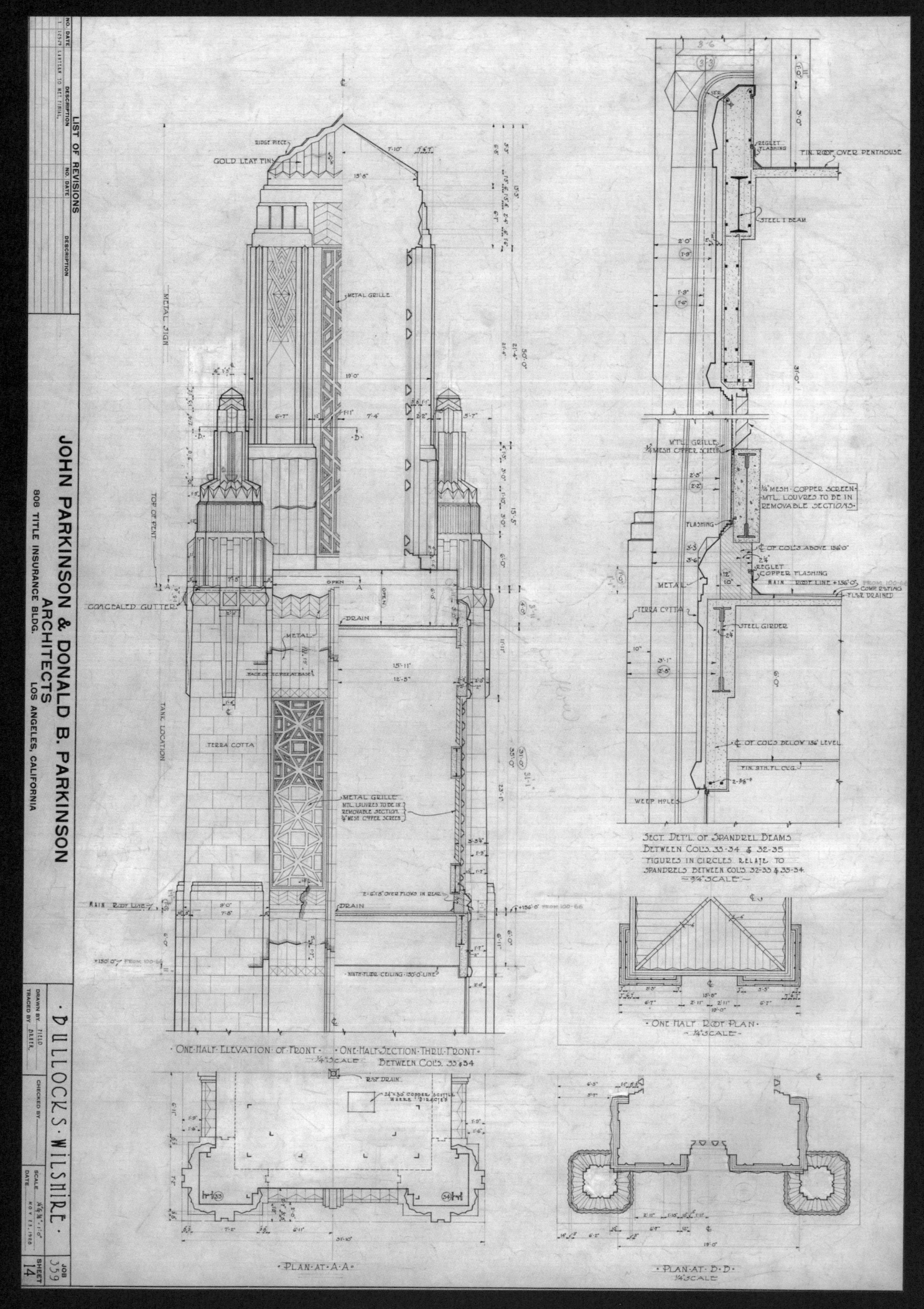

ICONIC VISION

INTRODUCTION

IF AN ARCHITECT DESIGNED MANY OF THE ICONIC STRUCTURES IN ONE OF THE MOST INFLUENTIAL CITIES IN THE WORLD, IT IS REASONABLE TO EXPECT SCHOLARS WOULD EXAMINE HIS WORK AND CELEBRATE HIS LEGACY. And yet, in Los Angeles, the city's greatest architect has been all but forgotten.

From 1894 to his death in 1935, John Parkinson created many of the important structures in the heart of the city: Los Angeles City Hall, the Los Angeles Memorial Coliseum, Bullock's Wilshire, Union Station, and many other well-known landmarks were all designed by John Parkinson.

More than seventy-five years after his death, these architectural gems remain a vibrant, integral part of the city's identity in the midst of a sprawling metropolis that has expanded ever further outward. However, there have been no books about his work freely available in the Los Angeles Public Library or any other library. There is no statue or street named in recognition of his contribution. And although he designed many of the most recognizable buildings on the campus of the University of Southern California, no academic course is dedicated to the study of his achievements.

John Parkinson's legacy is as important to Los Angeles as that of McKim, Mead, and White to New York City. Parkinson shaped Los Angeles's architectural identity and brought to life the bold ambition of his clients at a time when there were no limits placed on the city's expectations.

Unlike many celebrated L.A. architects who made their reputations by designing unique private homes for wealthy clients, Parkinson believed true architectural glory came through designing grand public buildings. He was prepared to compete with anyone to win a significant commission and ready to work without payment if a project appealed to his sense of civic duty.

When his son Donald joined the architectural practice, the elder Parkinson made it clear "great profits are secondary to good work." This standard guided his entire architectural career. Believing that the citizens of Los Angeles should be inspired by their surroundings, he championed regulations to beautify the city.

Parkinson's story is even more remarkable because it began in a small village in the industrial north of England. With only limited training, he became an architect almost by accident. His raw ambition and considerable charisma ultimately led him to a life that would have been unimaginable in his youth. That he would go on to design the most modern city in the world seems totally incongruous. Yet Parkinson always believed he could do great things.

When he published his autobiography for family and close friends shortly before his death, he largely ignored his own architectural achievements, perhaps taking them for granted. He left it for others to explain the details of his finest work and instead chose to focus on his extraordinary journey to becoming the head of Los Angeles's dominant architectural firm.

After he died, the *Los Angeles Times* compared his legacy to the architects who designed the Taj Mahal and the Strasbourg Cathedral. His obituary read: "John Parkinson of Los Angeles earned a distinction that death cannot obliterate. The passing years will bring ever-added proof of how much the city owes to his vision and his artistry."

This book at long last honors John Parkinson, whose life, work, and iconic vision deserve to be celebrated.

—Stephen Gee, 2013

TITLE
GUARANTEE
RENDERING

FROM THE GROUND UP

JOHN PARKINSON

MORE THAN ANY OTHER ARCHITECT, JOHN PARKINSON DEFINED THE LOOK AND FEEL OF LOS ANGELES AS A CITY LOOKING TO THE FUTURE. He was the dominant architect during a period of unparalleled expansion, a time when Los Angeles transitioned from merely an outpost into a major metropolis conceived to become the most important city in the United States. And yet, while many of his buildings remain an essential part of the city's identity, Parkinson's name and legacy have been all but forgotten, gradually buried with the passing of years.

Often viewed as a distinctly modern, sprawling, futuristic city, so much of what defines Los Angeles today came about long ago in the opening decades of the twentieth century. Urban planners and investors were attempting to build a new city of global significance on the west coast of America—and they were doing it from the ground up.

To be considered an important city, Los Angeles needed to look the part. So construction began on the city's first skyscraper, the Braly Block, in 1902, and was completed by 1904; the city's first world-class hotel, the Alexandria, opened its doors in 1906. Ground was broken for a major expansion of the University of Southern California in 1919. And, when work began in 1921 on Los Angeles Memorial Coliseum, the belief was that Los Angeles would become a world center of athletics. The creation of the Coliseum was directly linked to an ultimately successful bid by Los Angeles to host the Summer Olympics, only the second American city at the time to have won that high honor.

City planners realized that to be a great city, Los Angeles required a civic center where public buildings could be grouped to symbolize the heart of the city. What they couldn't agree upon was who should design its centerpiece, the new city's new City Hall. A bitter legal fight, in which two rival groups of architects were hired by different government agencies for the same job, dominated newspaper headlines, and captured the public's attention for months. Finally, it was the building from Parkinson's design that opened on April 26, 1928—and would soon become the icon of the city. The new structure was hailed as a masterpiece. More than five hundred thousand people lined the streets for its opening day parade.

Until this period, Los Angeles architecture had largely followed the popular design trends of the East Coast. As the city established its own identity, designers began to experiment with modern architectural styles. In 1929, Los Angeles witnessed the ultimate expression of what became known as Art Deco design in the form of Bullock's Wilshire, a department store simultaneously original, modern, and eye-catching. The building, itself, would also change the way America shopped by embracing a new type of customer, the motorist. In its heyday, Bullock's Wilshire counted among its patrons the likes of Marlene Dietrich, Alfred Hitchcock, Greta Garbo, and John Wayne. Because of the store's design, the French term *porte cochere* became part of California parlance and a symbol of the city's freewheeling lifestyle.

Work also began on the design of the Los Angeles Union Passenger Terminal, known as Union Station. Rival railroad companies so fiercely opposed the idea of a shared rail station that the project lingered in the courts for more than two decades,

Braly Block, John Parkinson's original renderings

Hotel Alexandria

Los Angeles Memorial Coliseum

Los Angeles Memorial Coliseum

making it all the way to the U.S. Supreme Court—twice. The station took so long to build that by the time the depot opened, the era of train travel was coming to an end as Americans increasingly chose to travel by car or airplane. Still, for many immigrants headed to California, it would be the first place they set foot when they arrived. It proved to be "the last great train station built anywhere in the world," according to architectural historian Thomas S. Hines.

Each of these distinctive Los Angeles landmarks owes its design to the same person—John Parkinson. The son of a mill worker, born in Scorton, Lancashire, England, in 1861, Parkinson arrived in North America in 1883 with little more than five dollars and a toolbox. His adventures would take him to Winnipeg, Minneapolis, San Francisco, Napa, and Seattle before settling in his adopted hometown, Los Angeles, in 1894.

Over the next four decades, he earned his place as the city's preeminent architect and would play a central role in defining a vision for Los Angeles. "The irony of Parkinson's career," USC architectural historian Kenneth Breisch says, "is that he created these monumental, iconic buildings and structures in Los Angeles that have come to define the city, but he was working concurrently with the darlings of architectural history and criticism: Richard Neutra, Rudolph Schindler, Frank Lloyd Wright. They are the architects who have gotten all the attention because they are modernists. None of them created the kind of monumental or iconic imagery that came out of the office of John Parkinson." John Parkinson's buildings are so entwined with the identity of Los Angeles that even if someone has never been to the City of Angels, he or she is likely to be familiar with structures he designed. The buildings have become part of everyday culture, immortalized on television and the big screen.

Los Angeles City Hall was used for the 1950s television shows *Dragnet* and *Adventures of Superman*, and was "destroyed" in the 1953 film *War of the Worlds*. Union Station was the backdrop for movie scenes from *Blade Runner* (1982), *Star Trek: First Contact* (1996), and *Pearl Harbor* (2001), to name but a few. Angela Lansbury, who had once been a shopgirl there, returned to Bullock's Wilshire to shoot two episodes of *Murder, She Wrote*, and the Art Deco wonder was also a backdrop in Alfred Hitchcock's *Family Plot* (1976), Warren Beatty's *Bugsy* (1991), and Aerosmith's *Love in an Elevator* 1989 music video.

The Los Angeles Coliseum remains the city's most storied sports venue, and the first stadium in the modern era to be used

ICONIC VISION

Los Angeles City Hall
construction

From the Ground Up

Los Angeles
City Hall

for the Opening Ceremonies and track and field competitions for two Olympic Games. It has welcomed two Super Bowls and a World Series, along with countless professional football, baseball, and soccer games, as well as many sold-out appearances by its current occupant, the USC Trojans football team. The Coliseum has hosted many historic appearances by the likes of John F. Kennedy, Charles Lindbergh, Franklin D. Roosevelt, General George S. Patton, and Pope John Paul II, as well as sold-out music concerts by Bruce Springsteen, U2, Pink Floyd, and the Rolling Stones.

Walking along Spring Street or Broadway in downtown Los Angeles, one can see a Parkinson building in almost every direction. As historian Kevin Starr explains, "John Parkinson's work is as alive and well as when the buildings were first inaugurated. If we come back to Los Angeles two hundred years from now, many of the buildings we see around us will be gone, but John Parkinson's buildings will still be there, they'll still be in productive use, and they'll still be beautiful."

BULLOCK'S WILSHIRE TOWER

LOS ANGELES UNION PASSENGER TERMINAL CONSTRUCTION

JOHN PARKINSON,
AGE 16

BORN IN ENGLAND

SCORTON

NOTHING ABOUT HIS HUMBLE BEGINNINGS HINTED AT THE REMARKABLE JOURNEY THAT LAY AHEAD OF JOHN PARKINSON.

He was born into a working-class family in the English village of Scorton, Lancashire, on December 12, 1861. His father, Thomas, an engineer at the local cotton mill, had lived in the area his entire life. "He was a capable man," Parkinson wrote of his father, "of strong character, but with keen sympathy and kindliness for all things living; never smoked or drank intoxicating liquors."

Parkinson's mother, Mary Ann, who grew up a street away, was a housewife, devoted to her son and his older sister, Margaret. "She was everything the word 'mother' expresses," Parkinson also wrote, "devoted to her children, unselfish and self-sacrificing, capable and courageous under all circumstances, and dependable in any emergency; never complaining, and like her neighbors, working hard, doing everything about the home without any help."

When Parkinson was three, the family moved to Swinton, fifty miles away on the outskirts of Manchester, when his father was hired as an engineer in a weaving mill. Swinton had emerged as an important mill town during the industrial revolution, and by 1864 it was booming. Parkinson attended school and church with his family, but by his own admission, he was not an exceptional student. "Drawing was the only thing I enjoyed and anticipated with pleasure," he later wrote. "Gradually there appealed to me as the only vocations worthwhile to be an artist or a joiner (carpenter)." Although his family never went hungry and stayed out of debt, Parkinson accepted that his parents could not afford to indulge his artistic ambitions.

In 1870, the family moved again, this time to Bolton, ten miles northwest of Manchester, when Thomas Parkinson was hired as the engineer for a newly constructed cotton mill. In the midst of a rapid expansion, the town had been an important center for textiles since the fifthteenth century, when Flemish weavers settled in the region. The Parkinsons moved into a terraced brick house in an area known as Victory before relocating to 50 Bashall Street, Halliwell, a house they shared with Thomas's brother, Richard, who worked at a nearby cotton mill.

Much of the young Parkinson's time was spent in the classroom; he attended St. Luke's Day School on weekdays, followed by church services and Sunday school at the Park Street Chapel. But on his thirteenth birthday, he left school behind and began his working life as an errand boy in a hardware store, where "when not delivering packages, he was kept busy sandpapering the rust off and keeping the hardware polished and clean." When his enthusiasm ran out, he quit and joined the *Bolton Guardian* newspaper, where for the next two years he delivered newspapers, swept floors, and performed other menial tasks.

In March 1877, another job opportunity opened up for Parkinson, one that he could not have imagined would dramatically change and shape the rest of his life. Welshman John Roberts, a local contractor and builder, hired Parkinson as an apprentice. Roberts was known for building stone houses, churches, and commercial buildings. "I was not a very strong boy; rather small for my age of fifteen years and three months, but found I had undertaken a strong boy's job," Parkinson recalled.

A newcomer to this world of building structures, the teenaged

JOHN PARKINSON'S
FATHER
THOMAS
PARKINSON

JOHN PARKINSON'S
MOTHER
MARY ANN
BIBBY PARKINSON

Parkinson became immersed in his new line of work. Parkinson's practical experience grew over time and so did his interest in the technical aspects of construction. During the winter months, he enrolled in the Mechanics Institute of Bolton, where he studied building construction and design. He also attended classes in mensuration and surveying at his former school, St. Luke's.

For a solid six years, he studied and worked, and by the time his apprenticeship came to an end, Parkinson had a good grasp of basic building techniques. "I could do anything in woodwork from rough carpentry to cabinet work," he proudly explained, "knew the construction of buildings from the foundation to the top of the highest finial, was a draftsman, too, an artist born, with confidence unlimited and trained to endure."

WINNIPEG AND MINNEAPOLIS AND HOME

Parkinson was ready for adventure, so together with his good friend Joe Glazebrook, he decided to head to Canada and meet up with Evan Hughes, a carpenter he befriended while working for John Roberts. Hughes now lived with his wife in Winnipeg, Manitoba.

"Clubbing our resources we had enough to buy emigrant tickets, our food on the way, and estimated there would be about five dollars each left in our pockets when we should reach Winnipeg," he later remembered. "It was a painful experience parting from our parents, and with sad hearts in March 1883, Joe and I, each with little else than a box of tools, along with about three hundred others, comprising Germans, Swedes, Russians, Irish, and some English and Scotchmen, boarded the old cattle boat, the *Prussian*, at Liverpool, and sailed down the Mersey, bound for Halifax, Nova Scotia."

Winnipeg was incorporated as a city in 1874, and its population doubled in a single year to twelve thousand after a railway connection was made to St. Paul, Minnesota, in 1879. In the spring of 1881, the Canadian Pacific Railway Company began a regular service to Winnipeg, and within a few months the population grew to twenty thousand. When Parkinson arrived in 1883, the city "had no paved streets—just rich, deep black adobe—sticky and impassable after a rain."

Shortly after their arrival, Parkinson and Glazebrook found work building fences along vast stretches of prairie in Kildonan, three miles outside Winnipeg. Living in a log cabin on the bank of the Red River, they managed to save the majority of the $2.50 they were paid daily, and by June they had enough money to begin the next stage of their North American adventure in Minneapolis, Minnesota.

IMAGINARY LAKE
PAINTING BY
JOHN PARKINSON
IN 1873

BORN IN ENGLAND

Park Street Wesleyan Methodist Church, Bolton

Minneapolis had incorporated as a city in 1867, the same year railroad service to Chicago was established. The forests of northern Minnesota were the source of a booming lumber industry, while the farmers of the Great Plains provided the grain that was processed in the city's many flour mills. In 1880, Minneapolis was the thirty-eighth largest city in the United States and boasted a population of 46,887. Upon arriving, Parkinson was impressed by the "beautiful streets and great buildings," but knew he needed to find work quickly.

Before the sun had set, Parkinson and Glazebrook were employed at the Johnson & Hurd sawmill at Third Avenue South and Third Street. Established in 1866, the mill was the oldest sash, door, and blind factory in the city, and it employed forty men, who Parkinson remembered as mostly Swedes and Norwegians. "They were hard-working, high-grade mechanics who learned their trades in the old country," he explained. "They came to the United States to stay and make fine citizens—clean, honest, and self-respecting."

The business advertised an extensive range of "sash, doors, blinds, mouldings, window frames, stairs, newels, balusters, and railings." Glazebrook was assigned to the door-making shop, while Parkinson worked in the stair-building department. "I was devoid of any experience in stair-building," he remembered, "but had studied the

JOHN PARKINSON BIRTHPLACE TODAY

JOHN PARKINSON BIRTHPLACE

ST. LUKE'S DAY SCHOOL, BOLTON, ENGLAND; JOHN PARKINSON, TOP ROW, CENTER

A Builder's Apprentice

Observing a Fight

John Parkinson's artwork tells the story of his journey from a builder's apprentice (left and above), to his adventures in Winnipeg, Manitoba (opposite).

AN INDIAN SCARE

theory of handrailing and was confident I could make good—and did."

After working at the mill for about a year, Glazebrook returned to Bolton in July of 1884, and six months later, after acquiring valuable experience working as the foreman of the stair department at another sawmill, Parkinson, too, made his way home. "I was again with my people," Parkinson remembered as he adjusted to his familiar surroundings after the long journey. Back in the embrace of his family, he quickly began looking to establish himself in Bolton. "As I returned with the intention of staying, I was soon at work as a carpenter," he wrote, "but discovered that I was not considered a fully competent mechanic, but only an improver. That is a stage between the finished apprentice and a fully matured mechanic, a period of three or four years, and in that time unable to command the maximum wage. This was galling to me after my experience of being considered good enough to be a foreman in the United States."

Parkinson's frustration intensified when he interviewed for a position as a stair builder at a firm run by the Marsdens, two prominent brothers who had attended Parkinson's same Sunday school years earlier. "He scoffed at my presumption," Parkinson later

RUNNING DOWN A CANADIAN TRAIN

BORN IN ENGLAND 25

wrote of his interviewer, "saying it was impossible for so young a man, and he knew my training, to be capable of filling the position as stair builder. I replied that I could do anything that anyone else could do in their establishment; that I had been a foreman in the United States in a mill which made a specialty of stair building, but he was incredulous and declined to employ me. I was disgusted and immediately decided to leave the country at once [for] anywhere a man, now turned twenty-three, would be given a man's chance."

By happenstance, on a visit to the Bolton Art Gallery, Parkinson's attention was drawn to a photograph entitled *View of the Golden Gate from Telegraph Hill, San Francisco*. It was an image that made such an impression on him that, within days Parkinson returned to the United States and a new life on the West Coast. "I had a very vague idea where it was, but knew it was in California, which I understood was a hot, tropical country where one had to be very civil to avoid being shot or stabbed."

SAN FRANCISCO, NAPA CITY, AND A NEW LIFE

John Parkinson arrived in San Francisco in March of 1885. At the first opportunity, he climbed Telegraph Hill and paused to take in the view he had first seen in the photograph thousands of miles away in Lancashire. "I was glad the Marsdens in Bolton had refused to give me a job because I was still only a boy," he remembered, "and on Telegraph Hill I stood up, feeling that I was there a full-grown man among men, with no curb on opportunity—in a great wonderful country—and I was glad to be there."

His search for work took him north to Napa, California, for a possible job as a stair builder at a planing mill. In 1874, the Town of Napa City had been reincorporated as the City of Napa, and considerable improvements had been made to the area's infrastructure, transportation, and social services. Mining was an important industry and brought immigrants to the city, and many of the important houses and businesses built in the area were paid for by profits from quicksilver and cinnabar extraction. The financial center of the city was located on Second and Main Streets and dominated by the Bank of Napa, founded in 1871 by

MINNEAPOLIS MILL DISTRICT

Hennepin Avenue, Minneapolis

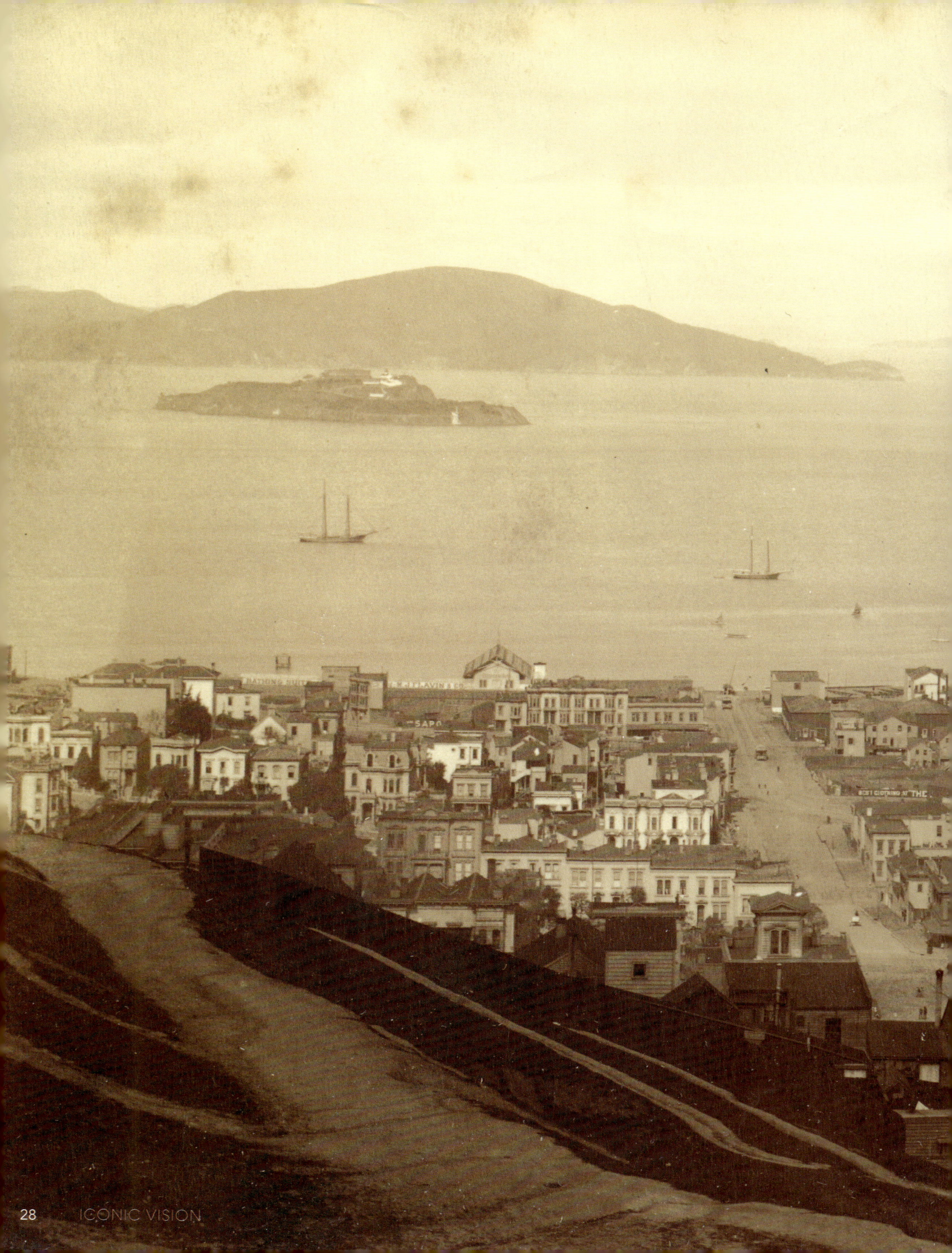

Parkinson headed to California after seeing this image, *View Of The Golden Gate From Telegraph Hill, San Francisco.*

Corlett Bros.
Mills, Napa

several local investors, including politician Chancellor Hartson. The region had also benefited from the development of the railroads, and while the population now exceeded four thousand, Napa maintained a strong rural identity. "In the streets were horses and buggies, men on horseback, farm wagons, and at frequent intervals, hitching posts," Parkinson recalled.

Parkinson was hired to work at the Corlett Brothers' Enterprise Planing Mill on Third Street. Each morning starting at seven in the morning, he worked a ten-hour shift, six days a week, earning four dollars a day. "There were neither unions nor Bolsheviks in those great days," he wrote. "The best man amongst the men was the man who could do the most work and do it well." He rented a room in a large brick boarding house owned by the Chapman family, who at first were reluctant to take in a male lodger but were won over by his youthful charm. "I knocked at the door. Old Mrs. Chapman partially opened the door and listened to my request," Parkinson later recalled. "She said nothing and shook her head, meaning no, but in the meantime looking me over keenly. An innocent looking young chap and evidently showing my disappointment, she asked me in and agreed to give me a trial."

Parkinson soon settled in. He joined the choirs at the local Methodist church and YMCA and, by his own account, became the most recognized bass singer in Napa. As his savings grew, he purchased a plot of land and borrowed funds from the Bank of Napa to construct a house he designed himself. Once completed, he rented the property and set his sights on bigger real estate investments. "I was feeling something of a capitalist and began thinking of places beyond the beautiful hill-bordered valley—for a new and greater field of operation—with the result that an embryo architect was soon to venture forth upon a trusting and unsuspecting world," he later reflected.

It was during an evening game of cards at the Chapman family home when the designs for Parkinson's new property caught the attention of Solon Chapman, brother of Asa Chapman, the head of the household. Solon Chapman was president of the Bank of Napa. "He and his brother Asa stood about five feet three inches high—two shrewd Connecticut Yankees who came to California in 1852," Parkinson remembered. "The Bank of Napa contemplated erecting a building. Mr. Chapman asked me if I could make the plans. I assured him that I could. A few days afterwards they had a directors meeting and appointed me as the architect."

While the bank was under construction, Parkinson formally entered two competitions to design a courthouse in the northern California town of Redding and a school building in Napa. Although he failed to win either job, this juncture proved to be a pivotal point in Parkinson's life; he was now convinced his future was to be an architect.

In October 1888, he traveled with the YMCA choir to Fresno for a convention. When asked by a local realtor what he did for a living, he hesitated slightly and then replied he was "serving as the architect of the building for the Bank of Napa, then under construction," although he was

STAIRCASE HANDMADE BY JOHN PARKINSON FOR NAPA BANKER HENRY BROWN

HENRY BROWN HOUSE, NAPA

BORN IN ENGLAND 31

ICONIC VISION

John Parkinson Designed
An Addition To
The Bank Of Napa,
On Right

A YOUNG JOHN PARKISON

JOHN PARKINSON POSES WITH FRIENDS IN NAPA

still employed at the Corletts' mill. This chance meeting led to a temporary position as a draftsman with local architects Snafel & Prawn, who were under pressure to complete plans for a new office block on Mariposa Street and Van Ness Avenue.

The new structure would come to be known as the Temple Bar Building. The architects had been recruited by investors S.N. Griffith and R.B. Johnson to design an elaborate three-story structure, providing space for both stores and offices. Griffith and Johnson had acquired the M.J. Donahoo Building in 1887, only to see it burn down the following year.

Parkinson stayed in Fresno for a week to create the elevations and was paid six dollars a day for his work. "My work with Snafel & Prawn was the only experience I ever had as a draftsman in the employ of others," he remembered, "and my experience there gave me considerable confidence that I could make good either as an architect or as a draftsman."

Parkinson returned to Napa, but it quickly became clear he would not stay. "The architectural germ was developing very fast and when the bank building was completed, I concluded to start out as an architect absolutely devoid of business experience, but knew that I was competent to make some sort of design for any structure that I might secure, able to take care of its construction, was confident and unafraid."

Yet, it was in Napa where Parkinson first met and fell in love with Meta Breckenfeld. The daughter of German immigrants John and Dora Breckenfeld, Meta was born in a working-class neighborhood of New York City in 1862, two years after her parents obtained their American citizenship. The family, which included two older brothers, Augustus and Henry, and a younger sister, Bertha, arrived in the city of Napa in the mid-1870s. By the time Parkinson arrived, Meta's father was well-established as a local farmer.

Their early relationship would soon be tested when Parkinson received a letter from a Napa family who had moved to Seattle. Their letter told of an exciting new city full of opportunity. "It occurred to me that it would be a good place to make an attempt to establish myself as an architect," Parkinson later wrote, "and on January 1st, 1889, I took my box of tools from the mill and, with all my possessions, boarded the steamer *Caroline*, sailing down the Napa River for San Francisco, there to take the steamer for Seattle. I felt sad as the old side-wheeler paddled its way down the stream. I had been happy in Napa, had many friends. Every day I had enjoyed the beautiful mountain-bordered valley. Why go to the rainy cold north to fight out a path amongst strangers in a profession where my competitors were educated and trained for the profession. How could I match them? But the paddles of the *Caroline* turned on, and I was on the way."

Griffith & Johnson
Block, Fresno

DAY SCHOOL BUILDING
SEATTLE
J. PARKINSON ARCH'T

B.F. Day School, Seattle; rendering

SEATTLE

SEATTLE NATIONAL BANK, DETAIL

"SMOKY OLD BOLTON (AND MY NEAREST OF KIN) WAS OVER SIX THOUSAND MILES AWAY, BUT I HAD SOMETHING BY NATURE IN MY EQUIPMENT, THAT NO COLLEGE OR SPECIAL TRAINING COULD PROVIDE: THAT FORCE OR QUALITY NECESSARY TO INSPIRE THE CONFIDENCE OF CLIENTS, FOR, NO MATTER HOW MANY OF THE WELL-KNOWN ARCHITECTS WERE AFTER THE JOB, I WAS ALWAYS IN THE COUNT AND OFTEN THE ONE SELECTED AND WAS SOON ACKNOWLEDGED AS ONE OF THOSE IN THE FRONT RANK."

—John Parkinson

JOHN PARKINSON LANDED IN SEATTLE IN JANUARY 1889, EAGER TO MAKE HIS MARK IN AN EMERGING CITY IN THE MIDST OF AN ECONOMIC AND POPULATION BOOM. It was raining when he arrived and "for weeks the weather was variations of fog, rain, and dense grey clouded skies, with scarcely a ray of sunshine," he noted. Although the weather was often gloomy, the outlook for commercial opportunities was much more encouraging. "The year 1888 had been a most successful and satisfactory one in all branches of trade in the Queen City," *Washington Magazine* reported. "Merchants were jubilant and hopeful, and the outlook for 1889 gave promise of a season of uninterrupted activity and prosperity."

Once again, Parkinson found himself in a new American city with no contacts and facing the daunting prospect of starting from scratch. "As I stepped ashore in Seattle in the first week of January 1889, long and thin, but strong and sound as a nut, tireless, [with] no business experience, an alien (I did not get my final citizenship papers until the summer of 1890), [I] was chuck full of confidence that I could do anything any man could do in the building line and faced the world without doubt or quaver," Parkinson later wrote.

In 1889, *Washington Magazine* described Seattle as "in the act of assuming its metropolitan robes, and discarding those of a thriving and prosperous town." The population was approaching 40,000 and would double by the turn of the century. The 1890 census recorded Seattle as the seventieth most populated city in the United States, and like other cities located close to natural and mineral resources, Seattle had a history of boom-and-bust cycles. In the years prior to Parkinson's arrival, huge improvements had been made to the city's water supply, sewage systems, and docks. Investors had begun to see the potential of a region that had been settled by pioneer Arthur A. Denny and his group of travelers—the Denny Party—less then fifty years earlier.

To succeed in his chosen profession, Parkinson would have to compete against Seattle's established architects, the likes of Elmer H. Fisher (who later would work for Parkinson in Los Angeles) and Pennsylvania-native William E. Boone, who had arrived in the Pacific Northwest in 1872. The influence of architect Henry Hobson Richardson, who designed prominent buildings in numerous cities in the East including Chicago, Boston, and Pittsburgh, could commonly be seen in the work of Parkinson's new competitors. "I certainly was the most handicapped of the lot," he recalled, "devoid of business training, unknown, [knowing] none in the profession— nor had I ever known any intimately, [with] no college training, or [any] association with educated business or professional men."

BUTLER BLOCK, DETAIL

BUTLER BLOCK

As architectural historian Jeffrey Ochsner explains, architects in Seattle in the 1880s and 1890s typically came from the building trades, and even Parkinson's limited instruction at Bolton Mechanics Institute was more classroom training than most of his competitors could claim. "He (Parkinson) was competitive with the other architects and perhaps a little better educated in design than they were," Ochsner says. "The design training they had gained was limited, and they really learned to be architects by becoming architects and doing architecture."

Parkinson made up for his lack of practical experience by closely studying the national architectural publications of the period and, whenever possible, integrating the latest design techniques into his work.

After renting a room in this new city, Parkinson set about trying to find a job and quickly discovered no established architect in Seattle was interested in hiring him. He decided to go into business for himself, leasing an office in the centrally located Squire Block and commissioning a two-foot sign displaying, "John Parkinson, Architect."

"With a pair of trestles, a detailing board, a couple of

Butler Block entrance

Competitive design for
Chamber of Commerce Building,
Portland, Oregon; unbuilt

drawing boards, a cheap wood chair, stationary, paper, and the old box of drawing implements I had used at school in England, I was ready to begin upon any trusting client," Parkinson wrote.

One of the first to walk into Parkinson's modest office was the Canadian contractor Weymouth Crowell, who quickly made friends with the young architect and alerted him to a new apartment development project, for which he was later hired. Soon afterwards, another chance visitor who noticed Parkinson's sign would become his first business partner. Englishman Cecil C. Evers walked in and introduced himself as a draftsman. Parkinson was familiar with his artistic talents, having seen a watercolor drawing Evers had prepared for another Seattle architect. Although he couldn't afford to hire Evers, Parkinson offered him the chance to join the business. They formed the partnership of Parkinson & Evers.

While Parkinson would acknowledge his new partner was a talented artist, he soon became frustrated with their business arrangement. "Evers had been with me but a few days until I found it necessary for me to pay his board bills and other expenses, even to the expense of entertaining his girlfriends, and in that way he was very popular," he explained. However, there was a positive side to Evers's charms, as Parkinson discovered when the two entered an architectural competition to design a new hotel in Olympia. Parkinson labored on the plans and designs, and Evers created the perspective before they traveled together to make their presentation to the competition committee. "The wife of the chairman thought Evers was a fine young man and immediately aligned on his side," Parkinson later recalled. Thanks to Evers, they won the commission.

By early summer of 1889, Parkinson had completed the plans for the hotel, and construction was underway. On June 6, he returned home from work in the evening to the sound of blaring fire alarms. It was the beginning of what would what later become known as the Great Seattle Fire, an inferno that destroyed the entire central business district. "In less than six hours' time, the conflagration had covered an area of 116 acres in extent and left total destruction behind it. Every wharf, every coal bunker, every business house, every mill, factory, bank, hotel, restaurant, newspaper, in fact every vestige of what had been that very morning a bustling hive of life and industry, was utterly wiped out—as if it had never existed."

Fortunately, the office of Parkinson & Evers survived, although drawing boards were evacuated into a neighboring alley as a precaution. The office was located in the Boston Block, one of the few brick buildings that remained intact in the midst of such

MARGARET J. PONTIUS MANSION, 1889

JOHN PARKINSON AND BUSINESS ASSOCIATES, 1889

GUY C. PHINNEY RESIDENCE; UNBUILT

COMPETITIVE DESIGN FOR SPOKANE COUNTY COURTHOUSE; UNBUILT

widespread destruction. As city leaders set about the task of rebuilding, it became clear Seattle's misfortune had provided the inexperienced firm an unprecedented opening. "Here was an opportunity for young architects, and we appreciated the situation thoroughly," Parkinson recalled. "We found, however, that the old and well-known architects there were favored, getting practically all of the work despite our efforts to get some of it."

Parkinson's breakthrough came when he was introduced to pioneer real estate developer Guy C. Phinney, who was looking to construct a $120,000 hotel and office building on the corner of Second Avenue and James Street. "He stood over six feet tall, had a long, curly black beard, a florid, full face, and black eyes, drank whiskey, had the reputation of carrying guns in both hip pockets, and swore freely with every remark," Parkinson later wrote of his employer. "Phinney employed me as architect, and as he never swore at me or shot me, and as we remained friends for many years after the building was completed, my work services must have been satisfactory."

The pressed-brick, granite, and terra cotta structure Parkinson was commissioned to design featured galvanized iron trimmings and rose four stories high on Second Avenue and five on James Street. His plans called for a music hall in the basement as well as space for several stores and offices. Phinney oversaw construction and traveled to San Francisco to purchase the ironwork and steel girders for the building. "This was a large commission equal to that of any of the established architects, and it really put Parkinson on the map and demonstrated that he could handle a large commission as well as any of the older more established architects," Ochsner explains. When the building was completed, Parkinson would move his own offices there. The building would also temporarily serve as Seattle's City Hall.

"Soon after the Butler Hotel was started, we got several other buildings, and by the middle of 1889, had quite a number of draftsmen and were thoroughly established in business," Parkinson wrote. "I found, however, that Evers was almost useless, knowing nothing of practical construction and very little of design, although he was a thorough artist, and could make very catchy perspective drawings."

In December 1889, Parkinson returned to Napa, California. On Christmas Day, he married Meta C. Breckenfeld at the Methodist church downtown, where he had sung in the choir. He returned to Seattle with his new wife and soon afterwards decided to end his partnership with Evers. He paid Evers $1,700 for his share of the business and wished him well in his endeavors.

HOTEL OLYMPIA
BUILT AT A COST OF
$100,000, 1890

THE SEATTLE NATIONAL BANK BUILDING
SEATTLE · WASH·

JOHN PARKINSON
ARCHITECT

Seattle National
Bank Building

THE SEATTLE NATIONAL BANK

John Parkinson's architectural credentials were greatly enhanced when he secured a coveted commission to design the Seattle National Bank Building on the corner of Yesler Avenue and South Second Street. A dozen architects submitted designs for the project, which became Parkinson's most important commercial structure and provided a significant opportunity to showcase his growing design skills and knowledge of architectural trends. Prior to the Great Seattle Fire, there were eight banks doing business in the city, but only one survived.

Parkinson's design called for a Romanesque structure with a pressed-brick, stone, and terra cotta exterior. Upon reviewing the plans, the *Seattle Post Intelligencer* predicted the six-story building would be "one of the finest in the city." The ground floor contained three large storerooms and the public offices of the bank, while a total of 136 offices filled the upper floors. Three passenger elevators and two freight elevators were installed, along with the latest steam heating, plus electric and gas fixtures. Parkinson was so pleased with the building, he relocated his offices there. "The structure was built partly over tide water and partly on dry hard ground, but it has stood without any settlement," he assessed. Parkinson had good reason to feel proud. For an architect so young and inexperienced, he had created a remarkable Romanesque Revival structure that remains arguably the finest example of the period in Seattle.

On October 17, 1890, John and Meta Parkinson welcomed a baby daughter, Mary Dorothea. By the following June, the *Seattle Post Intelligencer* reported Parkinson's work projects totaled $257,600. His most important contract was for the new $200,000 Seattle National Bank building, and his other work included additions to the Denny, Rainier, and Mercer schools. "In those days I was full of energy; upon hearing of any job I would immediately go for it and was generally successful."

As Parkinson's profits rose, he built his own house on a lot he purchased on Renton Hill. "The house stood on a high basement and when a strong wind blew from the Sound it would ominously shake," Parkinson explained. "One stormy night the house quivered as each gust struck. At about two a.m., I could stand it no longer, got up and spent the balance of the night bracing the basement story." Parkinson later wrote that he returned forty years later to see the house standing strong.

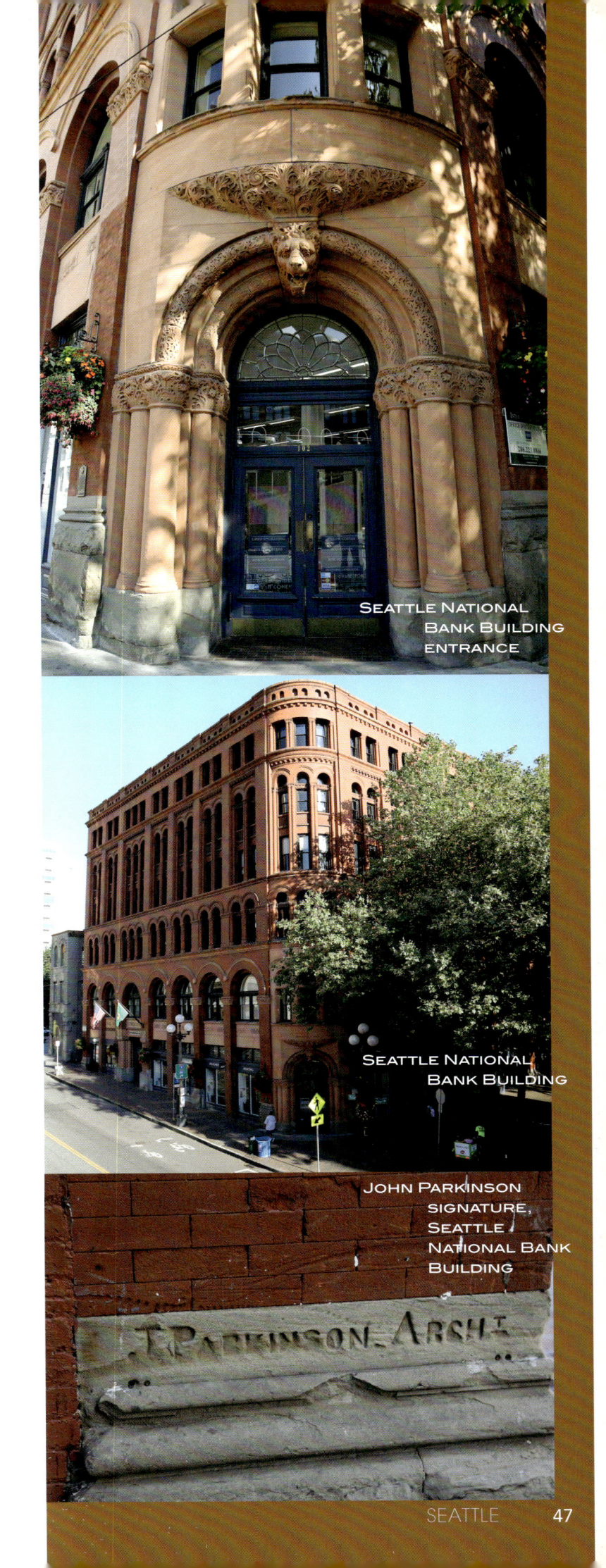

Seattle National Bank Building Entrance

Seattle National Bank Building

John Parkinson signature, Seattle National Bank Building

SEATTLE

J.A. HATFIELD RESIDENCE

B.F. DAY SCHOOL

PACIFIC SCHOOL BUILDING

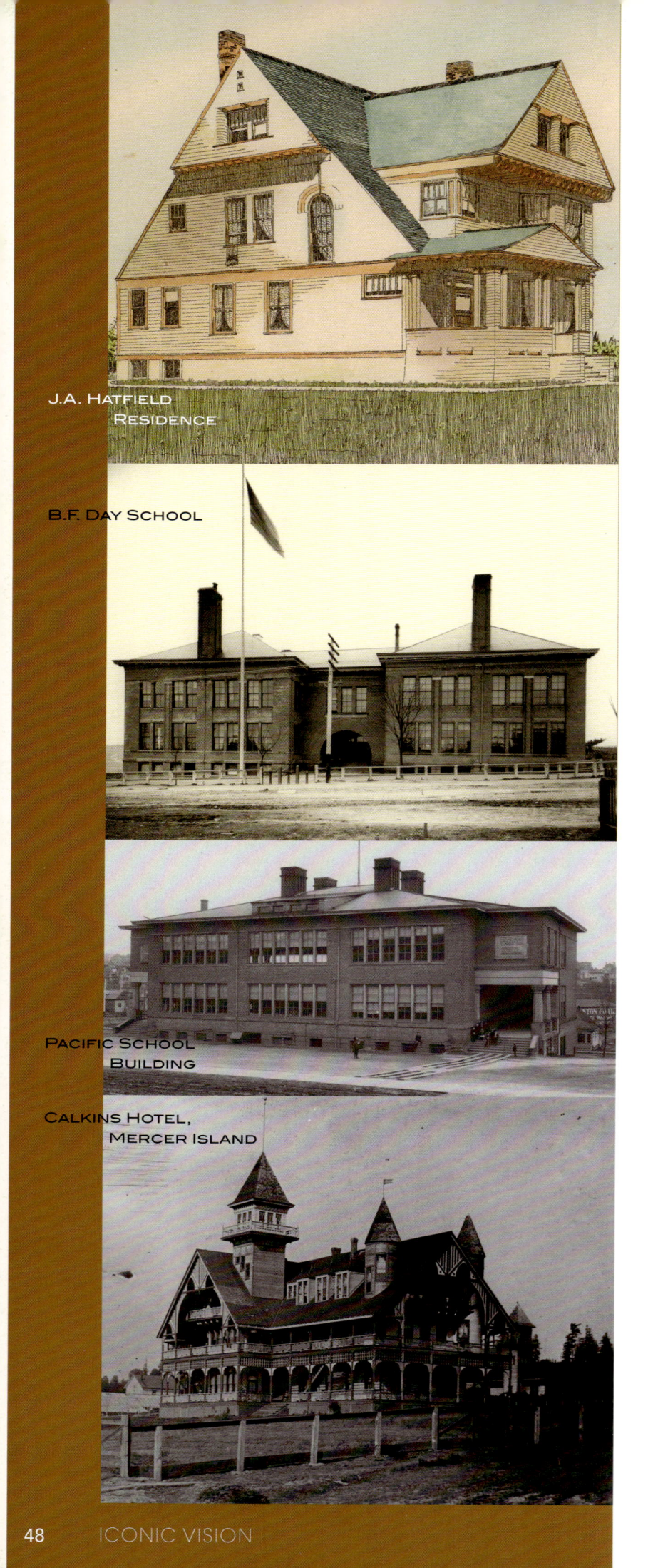

CALKINS HOTEL, MERCER ISLAND

BOOM AND THEN BUST

As Seattle's population grew, so, too, did the need for school buildings. John Parkinson emerged as the city's leading school architect in July 1891 when he won a competition to design a sixteen-room brick schoolhouse in an area north of Fremont. The Seattle school board received eleven submissions for the project to be built on land donated by real estate broker Benjamin F. Day and his wife Frances. The gift came with a condition that the school should cost at least $25,000.

Considerable newspaper interest in the project only enhanced Parkinson's public image, and in April 1892, he was hired as Seattle's first "Schools Architect and Superintendent of Construction." The position came with an annual salary of $2,500, a budget for office space, and an assistant. He was required to provide plans for all the school buildings and alterations requested by the Seattle school board. Creating the position of a permanent staff architect represented considerable savings for the board and job security for Parkinson but upset many local architects who demanded open competition for the work.

Parkinson was able to use his new official title to secure many more school projects in the region, including the Pacific School, Cascade School, Ballard Central School, and the South Seattle School. He later claimed to have designed thirty-two schools during his time in the Pacific Northwest, as well as a number of important college buildings, including the Seattle Seminary Building, the first structure built for Seattle Pacific University, and the Jesuit College and Church, the first building at Seattle University.

As his business grew, Parkinson invested in numerous real estate ventures, including a block of stone houses he borrowed $20,000 to construct and then traded as partial payment on four corner lots and a city dock that reached deep water. "On the Front Street lot I built a seven-story building, part hotel, and the lower portion for the Seattle Athletic Club. I also improved the dock for shipping, using eighty-foot piles," Parkinson later remembered. By the summer of 1893, he claimed he owed $150,000 in various real estate investments.

Seattle, like many other areas in the United States, was hit by a serious economic depression in the winter of 1893. Parkinson recalled, "There was neither business nor prospects. I was in a tight place." He struggled to sell off his investments as the real estate market utterly collapsed. He traded some of his properties for a ranch in Ashland, Oregon, but as his debts grew, and the peach crop failed, he was forced to sell it.

In February 1894, Parkinson was also forced to resign from

B.F. Day School
Entrance

SEATTLE 49

Dorothea Parkinson

his position as the architect and superintendent of construction of the Seattle schools or face the prospect of being fired. The board had failed in its bid to gain approval for $250,000 in new bonds to extend payment on its debt. Parkinson offered to work for a reduced salary of one hundred dollars per month, but the economic downturn meant the board could no longer afford his services. His resignation took effect March 1.

Despite the downturn, he remained philosophical. "I possessed to clean up my obligations, and then was worse off than when I landed in San Francisco nine years before, but had had some very real experience."

In one last roll of the dice, Parkinson entered a competition to design the administration building for the University of Washington. Although he didn't win, he was awarded a one-thousand-dollar consolation prize. "I got the one-thousand-dollar prize, took a trip to San Francisco and Los Angeles to look the ground over, with the result that I decided to locate in Los Angeles; [I] paid my bills and arrived in the city in March 1894, with fifty dollars' capital remaining with which to make another start."

·STVDY FOR THE·
·EQVITABLE·LIFE·ASSVRANCE·BVILDING·
·SEATTLE·

Jno. Parkinson · Architect·

Equitable Life Assurance Building; unbuilt

50 ICONIC VISION

Jesuit College and Church

Seattle Athletic Club Building

STATE OF WASHINGTON

·COMPETITIVE·DESIGN·FOR·
WORLDS·FAIR·BUILDING·
John·Parkinson·Arch't
·SEATTLE·

Parkinson's design for the Washington Building at the Chicago World's Fair of 1893 was judged the most artistic, yet was ultimately rejected because of fears the wooden tower would too easily deteriorate.

Los Angeles Municipal Arts Commission, John Parkinson standing right, 1902

LOS ANGELES

ENGINE HOUSE NO. 18, HOBART STREET

"How quiet and simple was life in those days of the early nineties: no airplanes, automobiles, radios, wireless, no movies or movie stars, no gangsters or kidnappers, no bootleggers, no Communists, or New Deal—a free country of free men limited only by their energy and ability."

—John Parkinson, May, 1934

John Parkinson arrived in Los Angeles in March 1894 with no contacts, almost no money, and a wife, child, and extended family to support. Like thousands of other immigrants who flocked to the city at the end of the nineteenth century, he was desperate for a fresh start and another opportunity to prove himself. Unlike the others, he now had experience as an architect and was determined to use it.

The Los Angeles of 1894 was hardly a sprawling metropolis. The 1890 census recorded the city's population at 50,395. while it would double in the coming decade, it paled in comparison to major cities in the East such as New York, Chicago, or Philadelphia, metropolitan areas with populations already at one million and growing. Los Angeles was further down the list as the fifty-seventh most populated city in the United States. But that was all about to change.

The completion of the Southern Pacific's Sunset Route in 1883 and the arrival of the competing Santa Fe in 1886 helped foster the belief that Los Angeles was a city worth investing in. The railroads relentlessly promoted the region's enviable climate and expanding business opportunities. "Los Angeles in the latter decade of the nineteenth century is a city bursting at the seams, not yet with people, it is not that big yet, but with ambition," historian William Deverell explains. "It views itself as the American city of the future and the American city of the twentieth century, a place with extraordinary ambition to supplant the power and influence of San Francisco, of Chicago, and maybe even of New York."

Los Angeles was "an outpost; it was a town en route to becoming a city," historian Kevin Starr adds. "It had only just begun the process of urbanizing its streets and its transportation system and its water system in the late 1870s and early 1880s."

The landscape that fifty years earlier had been dotted with whitewashed, tile-roofed, adobe houses was now dominated by an emerging city spreading far beyond its early plaza settlement. A decade earlier, Los Angeles's businesses began to expand south along Los Angeles, Main, Spring, and Fort (now Broadway) streets. With a few exceptions, construction was limited to modest two-story brick or masonry buildings with stores on the ground floor and offices upstairs. By the time Parkinson arrived, considerable architectural improvements were made, and a number of larger, wooden-framed structures, such as the four-story Hollenbeck Hotel, the Bryson Building, and the Wilson Building, had been built.

"The business center was from First to Second and north to Temple Street on Spring and Main, the better class of stores being on Spring," Parkinson wrote. "In 1894, Figueroa was the finest residential street of Los Angeles. Beyond Jefferson, a dirt road extended on through farmland to the sea. A few hundred yards beyond Jefferson was Agricultural Park, fenced in with a high,

CURRIER BUILDING

A.T. CURRIER

whitewashed board fence, and inside the fence, a double line of gum trees." Parkinson rented a cottage for his family on Pearl Street (now Figueroa).

He also selected an office space in the Stowell Block on Spring Street, between Second and Third streets, the same building that housed the Los Angeles Athletic Club. Strategically, Parkinson knew this would be a good place to make contacts. In those early days, his office was modest, as he later described, "Its equipment comprised a drawing table, T-square, etc., a set of instruments of fourteen years' service, and about ten yards of brown details paper whose surface was untouched but alert."

One of the first people to walk through the door was John C. Austin, an ambitious young Englishman from Bodicote in Oxfordshire, who was looking for work as a draftsman. "I liked his looks,—a square jaw; gray, intelligent eyes in which a twinkle hovered—a man to hold his ground and fight fair, asking nothing but opportunity, and, I was to learn, a man of courage and staying qualities, then about twenty-five years of age," Parkinson recalled. Although Parkinson couldn't afford to hire anyone, the two would become close friends and many years later would collaborate on high-profile projects including Los Angeles City Hall and the Chamber of Commerce building.

In his first month of work, Parkinson made thirty-five dollars, not even enough to cover the rent. "Following the depression of 1893, business prospects in the spring of 1894 were not encouraging in Los Angeles, especially for an unknown stranger without friend or acquaintances amongst the banks or businessmen."

THE CURRIER BUILDING

John Parkinson announced his arrival in Los Angeles in the Personals section of the *Los Angeles Times* on May 9, 1894. The copy read, "John Parkinson, an architect of Seattle, who designed many of the largest buildings in the city, has come to Los Angeles with a view to locating."

But just like Seattle, Parkinson again faced stiff competition from established local architects. The dominant firm in Los Angeles was Morgan & Walls, led by fellow-Englishman Octavius Morgan, Sr., who was born in Hothe Court near Canterbury, and John A. Walls, a native of New York. According to Parkinson, Morgan, who settled in Los Angeles in the 1870s, was "honest, outspoken, and

56   ICONIC VISION

practical, got the work, cared for it, and met the clients," and Walls was "the office man." The firm's many works included the Hotel Nadeau and the Van Nuys Hotel. "My advent in the place broke into their field of operation but we were very friendly," Parkinson later wrote.

Other respected architects included the all-German partnership of Capitain & Krempel and Robert Brown Young, a Canadian of Irish decent. Despite often competing for the same work, many of the more-established architects knew each other well and got together monthly for drinks at Al Levy's, a downtown restaurant.

Fortunately for the newcomer, Parkinson got an early break, thanks to a connection he had made in Seattle. Contractor Weymouth Crowell made the move to Los Angeles shortly before Parkinson, and the two reunited and teamed up for a project in Pasadena. Crowell had learned that the owners of La Casa Grande Hotel were looking to build an addition. The duo submitted a bid, won the contract, and Parkinson's run in Los Angeles began.

JOHN PARKINSON

LA CASA GRANDE HOTEL, PASADENA

LOS ANGELES 57

The Angelus Hotel was the tallest building in Los Angeles when it opened in 1901.

58 ICONIC VISION

Parkinson's enterprising spirit would serve him well when he soon discovered another potential lead. In late March, he noticed an old house being removed from a lot on Third Street between Spring and Broadway. "A man seemingly in charge, told me that the lot was owned by A.T. Currier who intended building," Parkinson wrote."

Born in Maine in 1840, Currier had served as Los Angeles County sheriff from 1882 to 1884. He was established in the local business community, and he planned to build an office building on his property. Parkinson saw the opportunity and won Currier's business by showing him photographs of his Seattle work.

To expand his business opportunities, Parkinson was clever enough to know that he needed to be introduced to some of the city's leading figures. On September 19, 1894, the *Builder and Contractor* reported, "J. Lee Burton, the well-known architect of Redlands, has moved to Los Angeles and joined forces with J. Parkinson in the Stowell Block." Seventeen years older than Parkinson, Burton was well established in Los Angeles

DONALD B. PARKINSON

CALIFORNIA CLUB, 1902

LOS ANGELES 59

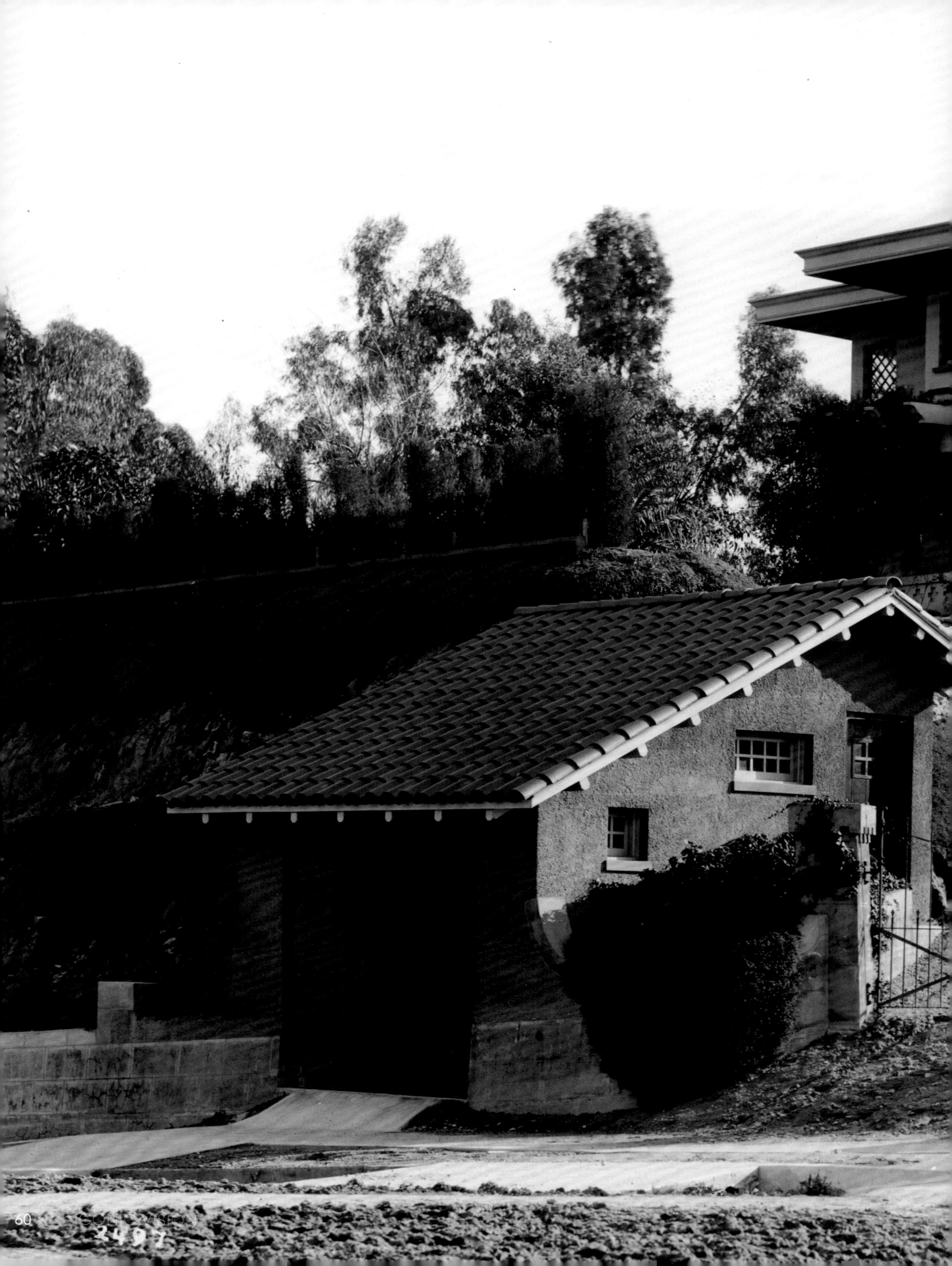
2497

John Parkinson
Residence

TRUST BUILDING

BOSBYSHELL BLOCK

and had previously been in partnership with Frank J. Capitain. It was a calculated move that Parkinson hoped would boost his standing. Although Burton's name would appear on plans for the Currier Building, it was Parkinson who led the project.

Burton was looking to expand his operation, and it wasn't long before the partnership of Burton & Parkinson unveiled plans for a host of new structures, including a $25,000 three-story commercial building on Broadway, a two-story commercial structure in Perris, California, and a two-story colonial house in Redlands, California. However, Burton's refusal to pay for a business license in Redlands landed him in court, facing a fine of twenty dollars. When he left without paying, a warrant for his arrest was issued. The police tracked him down to the Los Angeles office he shared with Parkinson and collected the money.

The early uncertainties of a new life in Los Angeles were now giving way to hope and a growing confidence for Parkinson. On August 10, 1895, he became a father for the second time, when Meta gave birth to a gray-eyed, brown-haired baby boy they named Donald Berthold Parkinson.

Construction was progressing well on the Currier Building, and Parkinson was beginning to feel more optimistic about his prospects. "As a matter of common consent, it seems to be conceded that the new Currier block on Third Street, designed by John Parkinson architect, now rapidly approaching completion, is the most perfect architectural production yet reared in the city," the *Los Angeles Herald* reported. "To be convinced that this opinion prevails, one need but to pause in front of the building for a moment any day and listen to the comment freely indulged in."

Parkinson's Italian Renaissance design for the Currier Building was inspired by New York architects McKim, Mead & White and Carrère & Hastings, whose work he followed closely in the architectural journals. The ground floor, dedicated to store fronts, featured carved dark purple Sespe sandstone contrasting with the creamy tint of the pressed bricks used on the four upper floors.

The upstairs offices featured the best and most expensive plumbing appliances and a combination of gas and electric fixtures. Although Los Angeles began generating electric power as early as 1881, it was still unclear which competing power supply would dominate the future. The building was fireproofed with terra cotta on all of the exposed beams and joints and featured the latest Sprague-Pratt elevator capable of running at 300 feet per minute with a load of 2,500 pounds. "In constructing the splendid block which bears his name Mr. Currier has given to this city a commercial structure second to none in the state," the *Los Angeles Herald* reported.

It was an establishing moment for John Parkinson who had made his first significant architectural statement in his new hometown. He would soon end his partnership with James Lee Burton and set up his own practice amidst the appealing aesthetics and modern conveniences of the Currier Building.

AN ELEVATOR OBSESSION

As John Parkinson's architectural career began to take off, so did another of his passions—his quest to develop a state-of-the-art elevator system. Any profits from his architecture practice were poured into perfecting prototypes of a working model he had first invested in while he was in Seattle.

According to his great-granddaughter Pamela Parkinson Kellogg, John Parkinson was "obsessed with the elevator" and prepared to gamble almost everything in the hopes of seeing a financial return.

"I had never seriously attempted anything in the way of inventions and knew little of electrical or hydraulic apparatus," he wrote. "However, I believed it was possible to devise improvements in elevator machinery, so each evening after work I would try to work out some scheme to make the elevator in which I was interested, a

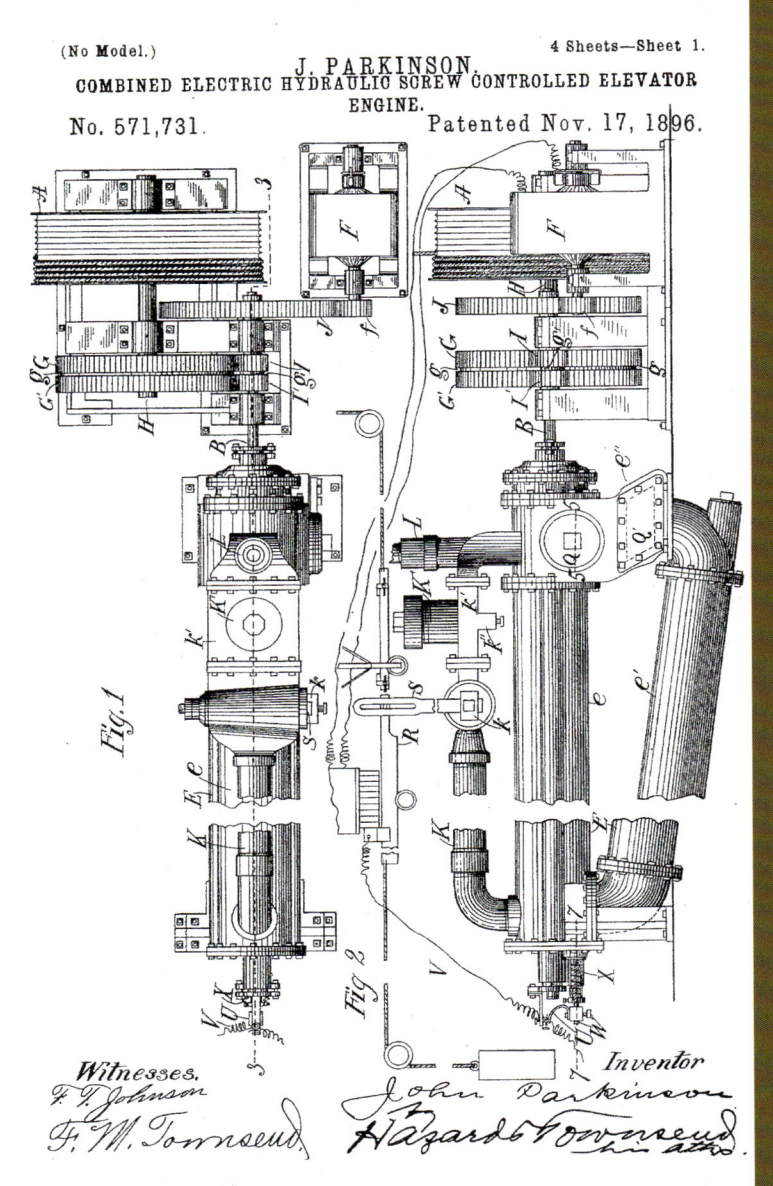

PARKINSON ELEVATOR PATENT

EDISON ELECTRIC COMPANY BUILDING

LOS ANGELES

HOMER LAUGHLIN

HOMER LAUGHLIN
BUILDING

HOMER LAUGHLIN
BUILDING
ENTRANCE

practical machine."

The first commercially successful "direct-connected geared electric elevator" had been installed in New York City in 1889 allowing for the construction of considerably taller structures. Parkinson knew that developing any major elevator innovation could lead untold riches easily surpassing anything offered by his architectural efforts.

He worked tirelessly to improve his device and by the end of 1894 had filed several patents and lined up investors who put up a million dollars in "paper capital" to help secure a contract for an elevator system in the Hotel Broadway.

Parkinson produced the mechanical drawings for the elevator, which ended up being successfully installed. "The peculiarity of the machine was that the hoisting motor was attached to the bottom of the car and worked its way up and down the shaft by means of pinions attached to the motor geared into vertical racks installed at each side of the shaft." By his own admission, it was "a crude and clumsy affair," but it worked "quite efficiently as to the use of power." Even though Parkinson himself designed the elevator, he never received payment for his work, but that in no way slowed his obsession.

In the years that followed, Parkinson was granted more than a hundred patents and relentlessly pursued his passion with zeal. In March 1896, an Associated Press dispatch from Phoenix reported the filing of incorporation papers for the Parkinson Elevator Company. At its first meeting, three officers were named: Dr. H.W. Westlake as president, Henry T. Hazard as secretary, and John Parkinson as treasurer. The new company's objective was to "manufacture and sell a new elevator operated by a combination of electric and hydraulic power."

"I was satisfied that I was off the right track for a really successful machine, and endeavored to find some means of a connection from the motor to propel the hoisting machinery which would eliminate friction and noise, and be an improvement on existing standard elevator apparatus," Parkinson wrote. "I thought that possibly some method could be used where the driving connection would be through water, something on the principal used in the centrifugal pump. Working along this line I finally thought of the idea of having an hydraulic attachment to the hoisting machine, so that the machine would run up freely by electric power and be lowered and held at stops by hydraulic means."

In addition to his elevator designs, Parkinson also took

ICONIC VISION

Homer Laughlin
Building
rendering

Parkinson teamed with architects Marshall & Wilson of Chicago to design the Mason Opera House on Broadway.

out patents in 1898 on a fire-protection system for buildings. He gave the trust on his newly built house to a friend in exchange for a loan of one thousand dollars, so he could go to New York and sell his patents for what he hoped would be a hefty sum. Parkinson traveled to the East Coast where he held meetings with the Worthington Pump & Machinery Corporation and Frank J. Sprague, who would sell his Sprague Electric Company to General Electric in 1902.

Parkinson told Sprague about his plans for a combined electric-hydraulic elevator. "[Sprague] said he was not interested in hydraulic elevators, that he was interested only in the electrical side, and there was no advantage in a combined electric-hydraulic elevator," Parkinson wrote. "In reply, I told him that I could do something that neither he nor anyone else had yet been able to do: operate a battery of elevators from one continuous motor, thus saving all loss in the resistance at the starting rheostat, and at the same time, have absolute control and safety."

Sprague carefully studied Parkinson's plans and, while he acknowledged the design would work, he insisted he was more interested in developing his own electric elevator system. After three months in New York, Parkinson's hard-fought endeavor proved to be a big disappointment. The only positive he could cling to was that word of the quality of his designs had reached both the mechanical and electric societies of America, which invited him to join their ranks. He left his elevator and fire-protection plans with a group of East Coast promoters and headed for home.

On the train ride back to California, reality began to sink in. "I realized that I had not received any money from the patents and that I had tied them up with people I did not know—promoters, that I had spent several years and all the money I could raise on the patents, that my house in Los Angeles was gone, and that I would be back in Los Angeles broke and without a job," Parkinson wrote. "I went up to my office, stayed there a while, then walked to the intersection of Third and Broadway, looked up and down Broadway, and realizing the situation said to myself, "henceforth I am an architect and nothing else, no more patents for me."

He had given it everything he had and only accepted defeat when faced with financial ruin. His pursuit had left him with all of

ENGINE HOUSE NO. 18, HOBART STREET

LOS ANGELES 67

STEARNS RESIDENCE
DETAIL

thirty-four dollars to his name. What saved Parkinson from economic disaster was a design for a starting device for electric elevators, "a magnetic control" that made it possible to regulate the elevator car even after it was restarted following a power outage. He sold the invention to the Otis Elevator Company for one thousand dollars and vowed never again to attempt to make money from patents, although he did design a speedometer for automobiles later in life.

THE HOMER LAUGHLIN BUILDING—
A NEW INNOVATION

The dawn of a new century was approaching and American cities were growing up—literally. New buildings in the big cities were getting a new look—they were taller with sizable frames made not of wood, but of heavy-duty steel. The use of steel-framed construction, in which a rigid steel skeleton supports the building's weight, began in Chicago in the mid-1880s, but it took more than a decade before the new technology was introduced to Southern California.

COLONEL JOHN
STEARNS
RESIDENCE

68 ICONIC VISION

Parkinson designed the Colonel John Stearns Residence in St. James Park in 1900.

LOS ANGELES

BERNARD RESIDENCE
DETAIL

John Parkinson welcomed the challenge of implementing this new technology and, in the process, would go on to make Los Angeles history. However, convincing ceramics tycoon Homer Laughlin he was the right man for the job was no easy task.

Laughlin made his fortune in East Liverpool, Ohio, but was set on living his golden years in the warmth of Southern California. He intended to spend his retirement developing Los Angeles real estate and purchased a plot on Broadway next to the proposed location of a three-story structure Parkinson had already been commissioned to design.

A veteran of the Civil War, Laughlin had a reputation as a tough negotiator—as Parkinson would discover in 1895, when they began discussions to build the city's first steel-frame, fireproof structure, an office block with shop space on the ground floor. Laughlin was thoroughly skeptical that any Los Angeles architect was capable of designing such an innovation, so he insisted Parkinson's plans be evaluated by an expert before any construction work was allowed to proceed. Parkinson agreed to the request, and his plans were sent to C.S. Pitkin in the engineering department of the Crane Company in Chicago.

BERNARD RESIDENCE

In the spring of 1901 John Parkinson designed a stone gothic house on Lake Street for wealthy widow Susana Machado de Bernard.

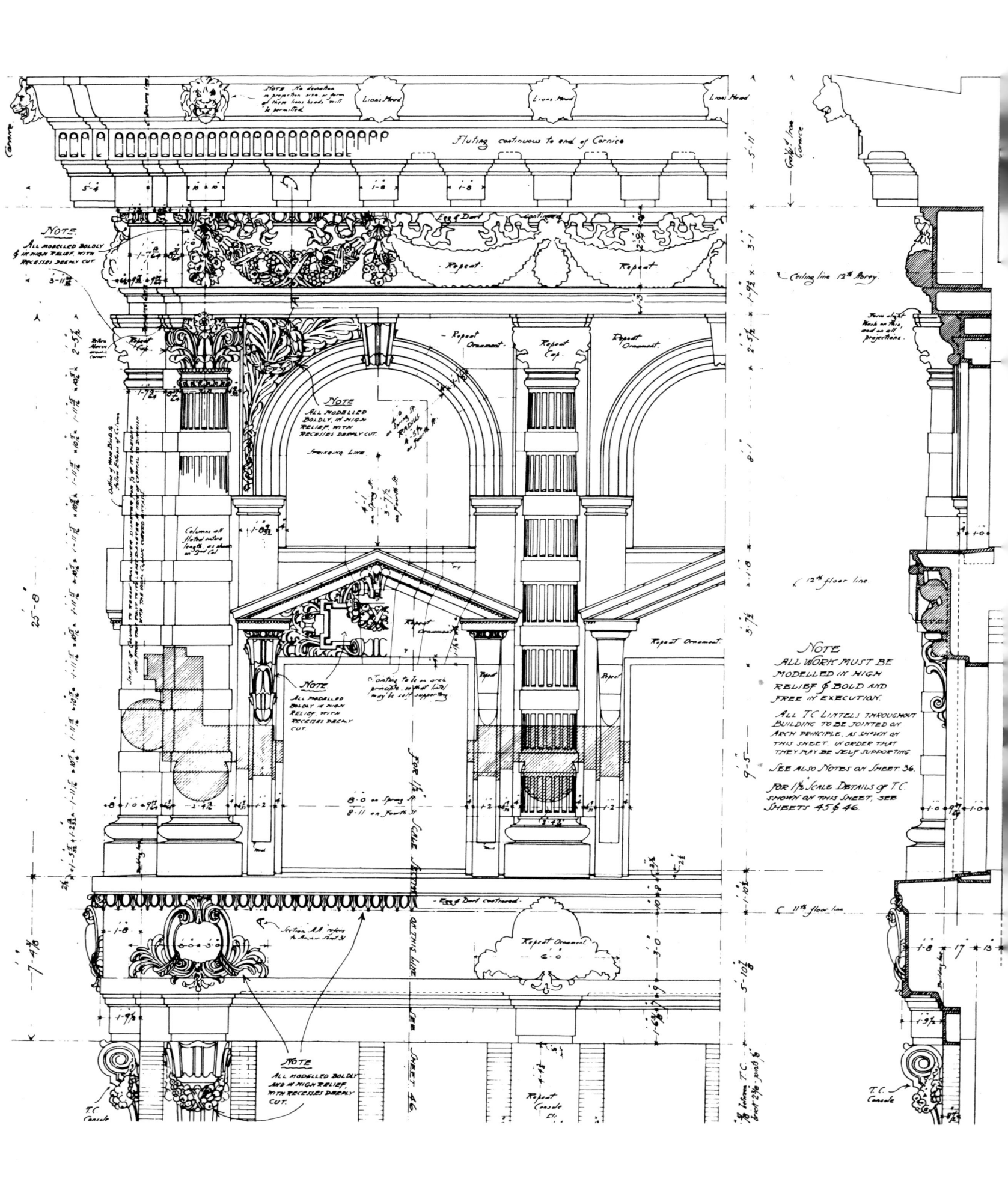

BRALY BLOCK, ARCHITECTURAL
DETAIL OF THE UPPER FLOORS

"In due time I received a letter from Mr. Pitkin stating that he noticed I did not claim to be a specialist in steel construction," Parkinson remembered, "that the plans showed the best arrangement of steel framing he had seen, and that he had so reported to Mr. Laughlin without any change. This resulted in me having a strong friend in Mr. Laughlin, who never failed to recommend me to anyone, thus establishing a reputation as an architect for large and important structures."

The Homer Laughlin Building rose six stories above its basement. Every effort was made to make the building fireproof: no wood was used in the structure of the building, and all of the finishing strips, doors, and window-sash casings were protected with metal. The floors were made of a mixture of Portland cement, sand, and cinder, supported by expanded steel, and protected by fireproof plaster. Parkinson even designed the riveted steel frame to allow for the possible addition of four more stories.

The building's exterior reflected Parkinson's desire for a simple-yet-elegant design. The main façade of the building was a cream-colored pressed brick, while decoration was mostly confined to the second and sixth floors where columns of terra cotta were used in the wide window spaces. Ornately carved granite columns flanked the principal main entrance. Directly above, on the third story, an elaborately carved scroll bore the trademark of the world-famous Homer Laughlin China Company, an American eagle subduing a British lion, symbolizing the battle between the established British ceramic industry and its emerging American competition.

Lit up by gas and electric light fixtures, the interior entrance hall was lavishly decorated with Inyo marble wainscoting while the flooring was a mosaic tile. Two of the newest electric Sprague elevators were installed, each capable of carrying four thousand pounds each. Antique brass was used for the elevator enclosures, light fixtures, and window casings, and the building boasted the latest plumbing and ventilation. In a sign of the progressing times, hot and cold water was available, and every room included a china washbasin.

The building's tenants also had access to a telephone connection in the main office. The city's first telephone company had been incorporated in 1881, and by 1895, the Los Angeles Telephone Company reported greater phone use per capita in Los Angeles than any other city in the country. Parkinson's design included a central courtyard to help provide natural light and ventilation to the floors below.

GRANT BUILDING

HOTEL MARYLAND, PASADENA, RENDERING

HOTEL MARYLAND, PASADENA

LOS ANGELES 73

JOHN HYDE BRALY

HENRY MARTZ RESIDENCE

BRALY BLOCK AT NIGHT

In July of 1898, the *Los Angeles Times* reported, "The approaching completion of the Laughlin building in this city will mark a distinct triumph in the building art of the world." The newspaper confidently predicted it would become "California's finest office structure" and heaped praise on Parkinson for his "knowledge of the latest and best works of American construction."

The Laughlin building now complete, John Parkinson became the first architect to design a Class A steel-frame structure in Los Angeles. In the years that followed, the use of steel would dramatically transform landscapes and allow the creation and bold construction of previously unimaginable structures in this city and others all across America.

The much-heralded Homer Laughlin Building, which housed an office for architect Frank Lloyd Wright in the 1920s, is now best known as the home of the Grand Central Market, the oldest and largest open-air market in Los Angeles.

THE BRALY BLOCK—LOS ANGELES'S FIRST SKYSCRAPER

In 1902, Parkinson was commissioned by a consortium led by pioneer John Hyde Braly, president of the Southern California Savings Bank, to design a structure on the corner of Fourth and Spring streets that reflected both the ambition of his financial enterprise and his belief in the future of Los Angeles. "The center of the business of the city was then at Spring and First streets—with a persistent southward trend," Braly later wrote. "This meant moving our bank nearly half a mile beyond the existing center; and reflecting the dubious opinion of the day regarding the future of the city, our board of directors (among the best and shrewdest businessmen of the city) stoutly opposed the idea—only to be later won over after much persuasion."

In July of 1902, Parkinson showed his plans for the classical Beaux Arts-style Braly structure to a reporter, and soon after, a headline, "Los Angeles' First Real Sky-scraper a Beauty" appeared in the *Los Angeles Times.* The accompanying article declared, "The new block will be a twelve-story structure that will be as nearly fireproof as architectural skill and modern appliances can make it." In the end, it would require more than a million bricks, 1,500 tons of steel, 450 tons of terra cotta, and six hundred barrels of cement to bring Parkinson's design to life.

Decorated with terra cotta arches and garlands and constructed at an estimated cost of more than a half-million dollars, the twelve-story, 173-foot-tall structure would house 209

74 ICONIC VISION

Braly Block

Braly Block,
roofline detail

offices, all with the latest modern conveniences, including three state-of-the-art elevators, individually controlled steam heating, as well as telephone, telegraph, and messenger wires. Braly's Southern California Savings Bank would occupy the entire ground floor. "The new banking rooms were the finest on the Coast; the twelve-story, fireproof, steel building set the pace for that class of structure in Los Angeles," Braly later proclaimed.

No single structure did more to enhance John Parkinson's reputation than the Braly Block. While skyscrapers were becoming more common in major cities like New York, Chicago, Detroit, and St. Louis, the construction of such an imposing structure in Los Angeles was headline news and viewed by residents as an important milestone in the quest to become an international city.

The *Los Angeles Times* was so impressed with the building, the paper's reporter exalted on November 22, 1903, "Six months ago there stood on the corner of Fourth and Spring streets, opposite the Angelus Hotel, a ramshackle frame building, a relic of the '80s. Today there rises from the same spot one of the finest structures that architectural genius and engineering skill can conceive."

Braly himself was equally pleased, "I knew that it was being whispered even among my friends that 'Braly's ambition had turned his head,' but instead of its being a merely personal ambition, it was really the outcome of my unbounded faith in the future of the city. In this case, 'Fortune favored the brave' to a certainty—for the results of the change were simply wonderful."

Parkinson had forever changed the skyline of downtown Los Angeles. As Scott Field, curator of the Parkinson Archives, explains, it would prove to be a seminal moment in the architect's career. "He had designed the tallest building in Southern California. Once that opened, that was his moment of glory, he was inundated from all sides for work." Historian Kenneth Breisch adds, "I think it was huge for Los Angeles to have a skyscraper certainly. It didn't put it on a par by any means with Chicago or New York or even San Francisco, but it was a step in that direction."

By 1904, Parkinson had relocated his architectural practice to the Braly Block, as did fellow architect Myron Hunt. It would remain the tallest building in Los Angeles for more than two decades, until 1928 when it would be surpassed by yet another Parkinson landmark—the new Los Angeles City Hall.

BRALY BLOCK, POSTCARD

MARSH BLOCK, PASADENA

LOS ANGELES

PACIFIC MUTUAL
LIFE INSURANCE
COMPANY BUILDING

PARKINSON & BERGSTROM

GEORGE EDWIN BERGSTROM

"IF THE HISTORY OF LOS ANGELES OF THE OLDEN TIME HAS BEEN SKETCHED ABOVE, THEN THE HISTORY OF MODERN LOS ANGELES FOLLOWS THE LIST OF BUILDINGS PLANNED BY JOHN PARKINSON AND BUILT UNDER HIS SUPERVISION."
—*Los Angeles Times,* April 27, 1912

LIFE WAS ABOUT TO CHANGE FOR JOHN PARKINSON WHEN AN AMBITIOUS YOUNG ARCHITECT, CARRYING A LETTER OF REFERRAL FROM ONE OF THE MOST RESPECTED MEN IN LOS ANGELES, ARRIVED AT HIS OFFICE IN 1902. George Edwin Bergstrom had arrived in Los Angeles in November of 1901 looking to make his mark as an architect. When he walked into Parkinson's office in the Homer Laughlin Building with a letter of recommendation from Edwin T. Earle, editor and publisher of the *Los Angeles Evening Express,* Parkinson hired him on the spot as a draftsman. It soon became clear the new employee, who preferred to be known as Edwin Bergstrom, had much bigger plans than simply playing a supporting role. Parkinson and Bergstrom would eventually form an alliance, and over the course of a decade-long partnership, the duo would re-invent the downtown business district—and forever change the Los Angeles skyline.

Born in 1876 to a middle-class family in Neenah, Wisconsin, Bergstrom's formal education markedly contrasted with Parkinson's more practical experience. A graduate of the Massachusetts Institute of Technology, he received formal architectural training at the Philips Academy at Andover and Yale University's Sheffield Scientific School. His first experience as an architect was working for Tower and Wallace Architects and Engineers in New York. However, much like Parkinson, Bergstrom's early education included comprehensive training in the operation of sawmills.

"John Parkinson hired my grandfather because he was a very well-educated young man," Bergstrom's granddaughter Anne Neblett explains. "The two men had a similar upbringing: they both worked in a mill company. My grandfather worked for his father and uncle in the Bergstrom Stove & Plow Company, and John Parkinson worked in a mill company as a stair builder."

Bergstrom's prospects improved dramatically when he married into a wealthy Neenah, Wisconsin, family who were making California their home. On May 15, 1903, he wed Nancy E. Kimberly, the daughter of J. Alfred Kimberly, one of the founders of the Kimberly-Clark Corporation. Since 1899, the Kimberly family had spent their winters in Redlands, California, and in 1905, they made the move permanent with the purchase of a seven-thousand-square-foot chateau. The same year, Bergstrom bought into a ten-year partnership with Parkinson, with the agreement that the firm would be known as Parkinson & Bergstrom. Parkinson didn't need a partner for financial reasons, but it is likely Bergstrom paid a hefty fee for his sudden rise in status.

Together, the architects occupied an impressive suite of offices in the Braly Block skyscraper. "The Parkinson & Bergstrom office is probably the largest west of Chicago," the *Los Angeles Herald* reported. "They have a great deal of influence in directing architectural styles in the city, and much of our boasted up-to-dateness is the result of their work. Messrs. Parkinson & Bergstrom

HOTEL ALEXANDRIA, UNDER CONSTRUCTION

JOHN PARKINSON

are progressive and public spirited men, thoroughly interested in whatever pertains to the public welfare." *The American Architect and Building News* added, "The senior member of the firm has been for years identified with the growth of this city and has supervised the erection of many of the finest buildings to be found in the business and resident districts. Mr. Bergstrom, with whom Mr. Parkinson has formed a partnership, is a practical architect of wide experience."

HOTEL ALEXANDRIA

The Parkinson & Bergstrom partnership began with making plans for the most palatial hotel in Los Angeles history: Hotel Alexandria.

Parkinson had designed many hotels, both by himself and in partnership with others, but none captured the public's imagination quite like the Alexandria. When it opened in 1906, city boosters trumpeted it as one of the most spectacular hotels ever built anywhere in the world. Its lavishly decorated interior and state-of-the-art amenities made it a popular destination for visiting dignitaries and the place to be seen for show-business celebrities.

Two years prior, real-estate developers, Albert C. Bilicke and Robert A. Rowan, recruited Parkinson to design a hotel on the southwest corner of Fifth and Spring streets. They envisioned an exquisite architectural jewel that would rival the opulent Palace Hotel in San Francisco and set a new standard for highest-class luxury accommodations on the West Coast.

A native of Coos County, Oregon, Albert C. Bilicke cut his teeth in the hotel business, managing guesthouses in the Arizona towns of Florence and Tombstone. His partner Robert A. Rowan was born in Chicago and raised in Pasadena, California. He began his working life trading goods in New York City before returning to Los Angeles in 1897 to begin a career in real estate. In 1903, the two men formed the Bilicke-Rowan Fireproof Building Company to develop the many sites they and their associates had acquired in the city's business district.

The Hotel Alexandria was projected to cost eight hundred thousand dollars and was to be built on land leased for fifty years from investor Harry L. Alexander. To make sure it lived up to all expectations, Parkinson embarked on an extensive tour of major East Coast cities to study the latest advances in hotel design. Upon his return, the firm of Parkinson & Bergstrom created elaborate plans for a Spanish Renaissance-style structure that would stretch

ICONIC VISION

Hotel Alexandria

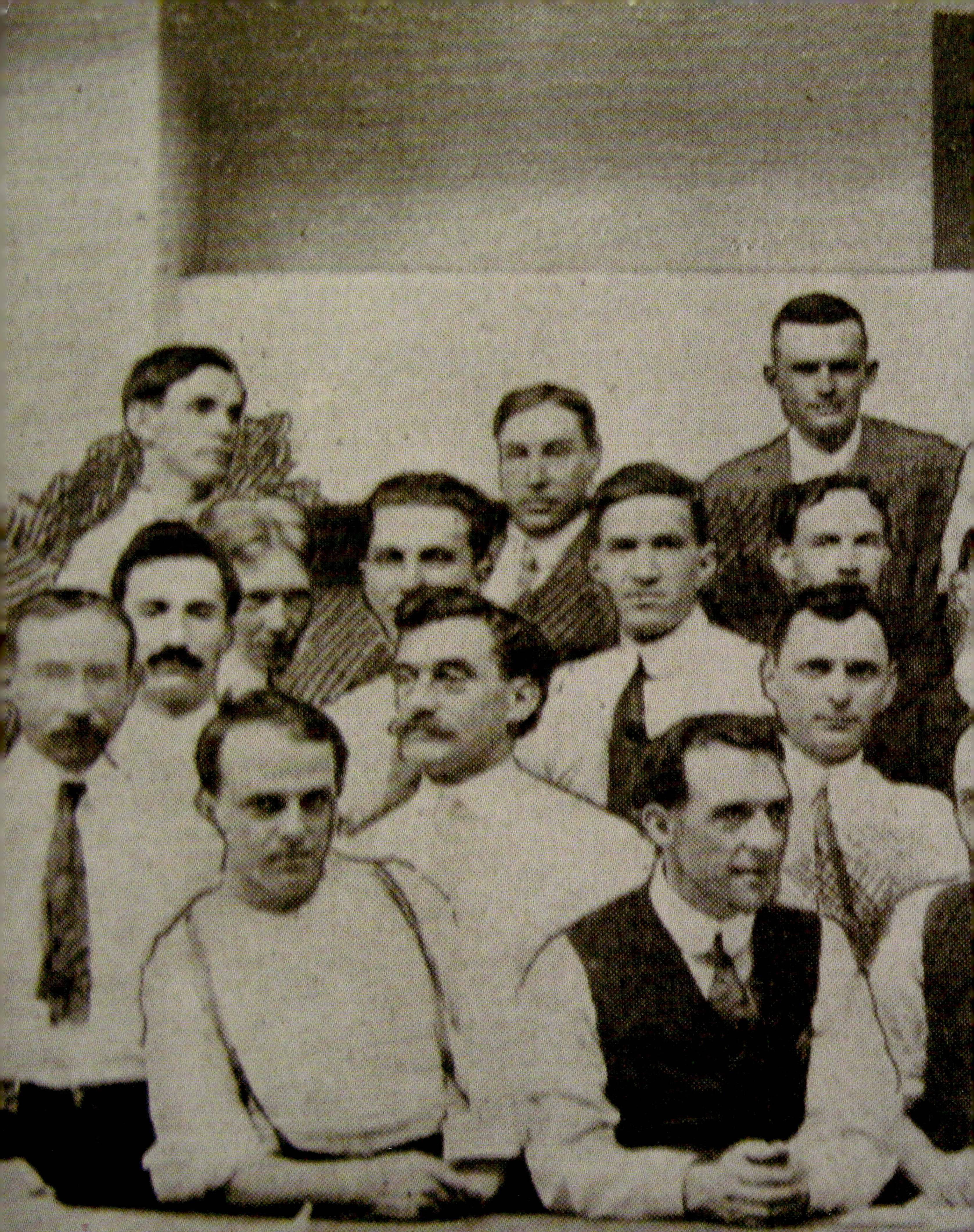

Parkinson & Bergstrom's team of draftsmen

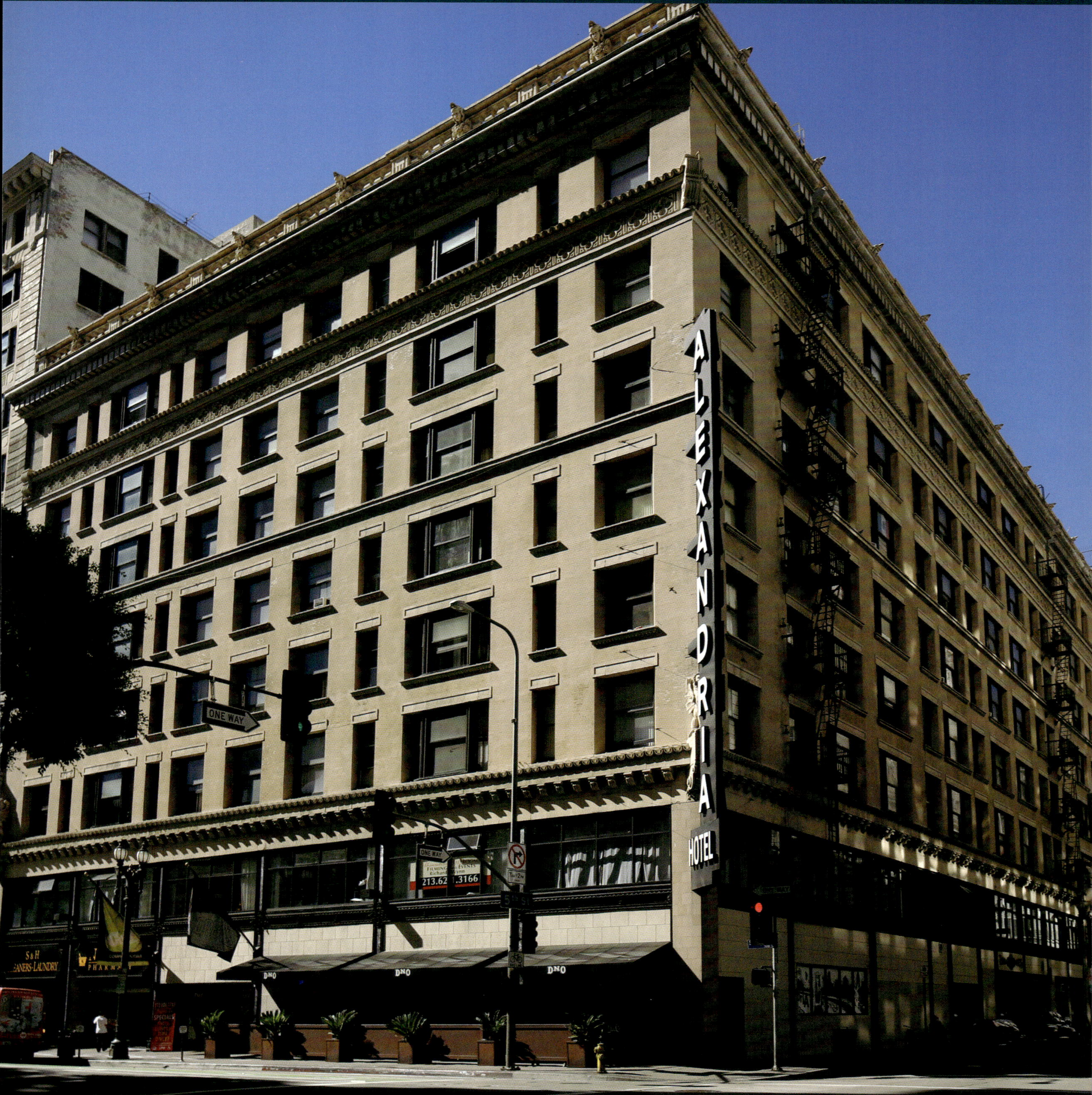
ALEXANDRIA
HOTEL
ONE WAY
DNO

160 feet across Fifth Street and 120 feet on Spring Street and house 360 of the finest guestrooms the city had ever seen. At full capacity, the hotel would accommodate five hundred guests.

When construction began, large crowds gathered outside to watch, encouraged by local newspaper reports heralding the hotel as a landmark development in the city's seemingly relentless expansion. Parkinson & Bergstrom worked closely with the Corona-based Pacific Clay Manufacturing Company, which produced more than a million Hollow Fire Clay Blocks used in partition walls, across the building's steel frame, and in the construction of the floors. "The destruction of Hotel Alexandria by flames is absolutely impossible," the *Los Angeles Herald* reported.

As the building neared completion in November 1905, the *Los Angeles Times* proclaimed, "Architect John Parkinson has given Los Angeles a hotel building that is without peer on the Coast or in the West." By February, a small army of workers toiled around the clock putting the finishing touches on a structure now with a revised estimated cost of two million dollars.

When the Hotel Alexandria was completed, newspaper reporters stood on the rich mosaic floor of the grand lobby and marveled at a series of sixty-foot stately pillars supporting an elaborately decorated balcony. They gazed in wonder at the elaborate decoration in tones of gold, green, and ivory, and gushed at the sheer expense of the walls that featured the finest Italian marble wainscoting.

The mezzanine floor, the promenade balcony, the ladies' parlor, and the hotel library beckoned to be explored. On the ground floor, the main restaurant, finished in fumed oak and Italian marble, had thirty-foot ceilings and elaborate glass chandeliers. The second-floor banquet hall, decorated in ivory and gold, contained private rooms where business leaders could meet behind closed doors. The *Los Angeles Herald* reported that the hotel's interior furnishings and decorations alone, selected and installed under the supervision of the Los Angeles-based Barker Brothers furniture company, cost three hundred thousand dollars.

HOTEL ALEXANDRIA LOBBY

KING EDWARD HOTEL POSTCARD

KING EDWARD HOTEL, INTERIOR

SOUTHLAND HOTEL, DALLAS, TEXAS

The hotel officially opened with fanfare on February 10, 1906, with some five thousand visitors on hand eager to see what all the fuss was about. The *Los Angeles Herald* reported, "The hotel was ablaze from top to bottom with electric lights and fairy lamps and the soft glow from the delicately shaded globes fell upon the magnificent Fresno work of the walls, ceilings and arches and made one wonder if he was not in a fairyland." S.J. Whitmore, the hotel's manager, told a crowd of gathered dignitaries, which included John and Meta Parkinson, "The building of the hotel has been one of marvel and speed and competency. The building is absolutely fireproof, and we have spared no cost to make it so."

Connected to the guest rooms were two hundred bathrooms with both hot and cold water. Modern steam heaters would keep guests comfortable during cold winter nights. The Los Angeles firm Putnam & Valentine provided photographs of western scenes that adorned the walls, while floors were elegantly carpeted with Oriental rugs, individually chosen to coordinate with the draperies and wall coverings. The more extravagant rooms were decorated in Louis XIV, Sheridan, and Colonial styles, and included furniture made of Toona mahogany and French walnut. All rooms were fitted with ball-bearing doorknobs to help reduce noise, as well as a newly developed locking system allowing staff to know if a room was occupied without disturbing guests.

During the day, the hotel's elaborately designed dining hall and public spaces became popular haunts for the movers and shakers of Los Angeles, while after dark, the café (which stayed open until after midnight) was an inviting place to dine for the theater crowd. Behind the scenes, the kitchens were fitted with the latest catering appliances, including an elaborate dish-washing system that relied on a complicated network of kettles and dish trays.

The hotel had barely opened for business before discussions were underway about how to expand it. Parkinson & Bergstrom was hired to work on various designs for Bilicke and Rowan, whose ambition to grow the property was restrained only by their ability to acquire the land surrounding it. Once they secured a long-term lease on an adjoining plot on Spring Street, they pushed forward with plans to build a twelve-story, $2,500,000 annex.

Seeking inspiration, Parkinson announced in November of 1909 that he would embark on a three-week research trip with

Albert C. Bilicke to Kansas City, St. Louis, Buffalo, Chicago, Philadelphia, and New York, leaving Bergstrom in charge of their busy practice. Parkinson's relationship with Bilicke and Rowan was a close one; they asked him to design all four of their properties at the corner of Fifth and Spring streets. In addition to the Hotel Alexandria, Parkinson & Bergstrom designed the Citizen's National Bank Building (Crocker Bank Building), Title Insurance Building (Rowan Building), and the Security Building as well. It was a successful run that, unfortunately, ended in tragedy.

"One day early in 1915, I was in Mr. Bilicke's office in the Alexandria," Parkinson remembered. "I designed several buildings for him and had known Bilicke for many years, very intimately; a hard-working, nervous man, going into fussing over every detail, checking up each night every item of the day's expense which must balance to the last penny before he could sleep. He told me that he was not feeling well. I advised him to quit worrying about so many things, others could attend to them, why not get something out of life? He replied that he was going to, and started off for a trip in a few days. About ten days afterwards, he went down on the *Lusitania* (ship), off the coast of Ireland. Mrs. Bilicke was saved. Mr. Bilicke was one of the men who did a big share in building the business section in Los Angeles."

Bilicke and Rowan's Hotel Alexandria, designed by John Parkinson and Edwin Bergstrom, would go on to hold a special place in Los Angeles history. U.S. presidents, royalty, and film stars all came to partake of its splendor. Among the many famous people who visited and experienced its unprecedented luxury were Presidents William Howard Taft, Theodore Roosevelt, and Woodrow Wilson; royalty, including the Duke of Windsor (King Edward III); as well as entertainers, such as Enrico Caruso and Sarah Bernhardt. In 1919, Charlie Chaplin, Mary Pickford, Douglas Fairbanks, and D.W. Griffith famously met in the hotel and struck up an agreement to form United Artists. Chaplin later got caught up in a fight in the hotel lobby with Louis B. Mayer, manager for actresses Anita Stewart and Mildred Harris Chaplin, from whom the actor was separated. A handsome young Italian actor named Rodolpho d'Antongulia was a regular at the tea dances before finding fame as the legendary Rudolph Valentino.

The hotel changed ownership in 1919, and several years later in 1923, the lavish Biltmore Hotel opened as the largest hotel west of Chicago. The Alexandria struggled to compete without lasting success and slipped into decline. The building was sold again in 1927. The decline of the Alexandria accelerated during the Great

ICONIC VISION

Fifth Street, Los Angeles, view shows the King Edward Hotel and the Rosslyn Hotel and Annex.

LOS ANGELES
ATHLETIC CLUB

Depression of the 1930s, and the property was sold yet again. In 1932, the Alexandria Hotel Company went into bankruptcy and was acquired by Spring Street Properties, which then sold the property to Federated Realty Co., Ltd., in 1933. The following year, Federated Realty went into receivership and sold off much of the hotel's glamorous décor, including a five-thousand-dollar chandelier and the celebrated Turkish carpeting, to help pay off debts. The sheets of gold-leaf covering on the mezzanine lobby walls and ceilings were stripped and sold for fifty thousand dollars. With much of the interior gutted, the hotel closed shortly afterwards.

In 1937, movie producer Phil Goldstone paid three hundred thousand dollars to acquire the hotel, and during the war years, the building enjoyed a short-lived revival. In the 1950s and '60s, the once-palatial Alexandria became known for its inexpensive rooms, and in the decades since, the property has been remodeled and revitalized numerous times, but has yet to regain the dazzling sparkle of its youth.

LOS ANGELES
ATHLETIC CLUB

A UTAH LANDMARK

As John Parkinson's architecture business grew, so too did his confidence in his young business partner, Edwin Bergstrom. Parkinson relied on his partner to take charge while he was away enjoying lengthy vacations with his family or working outside of Los Angeles. It was during one such family excursion in 1906 when an important client, angered by his absence, threatened to fire Parkinson unless he cut short his European adventure.

John Parkinson, his wife, and two children were enjoying a relaxing trip through England, Scotland, Holland, and eventually Kappeln, Germany, where Meta's mother had grown up, when an ultimatum arrived from financier Edwin T. Earle. After making a fortune in the fruit-shipping business, Edwin Tobias Earle turned his attention to Los Angeles real estate and became one of the area's biggest investors.

"As our steamer was secured to the dock, a cablegram was handed to me," Parkinson recalled. "It was from E.T. Earle, Los Angeles, demanding that I immediately return and attend to his building or lose the job. As I had left Bergstrom, my partner, in charge, it was being taken care of, but I wired Earle I would start back in ten days." Parkinson made good on his promise and returned to Los Angeles to take care of business with his important yet demanding client. However, it wasn't long before Parkinson would once again leave Bergstrom in charge. Former United States Senator Thomas Kearns commissioned the firm to design a landmark structure in the heart of Salt Lake City, so Parkinson packed his bags and headed for Utah.

After his brief political career ended in 1905, Senator Kearns shifted his attention to developing real estate. The following year, he invited Parkinson to design a ten-story office block on Main Street, the city's most important commercial thoroughfare. Parkinson described Kearns as "a big-chested man" who was "a fine sample of a fighting Irishman, a thorn to the Mormons of Utah." He added, "The Mormons respected him, however, as one of the strongest, outspoken and capable men of Utah."

Since the first pioneer settlements in 1847, the people of Salt Lake City had striven to establish a self-sufficient Mormon community, but by the dawn of the twentieth century, this vision had largely been abandoned as the city embraced capitalism. When Parkinson arrived, Salt Lake was undergoing some of the most dramatic changes of any city in the United States.

"There can be no possible question as to the future greatness

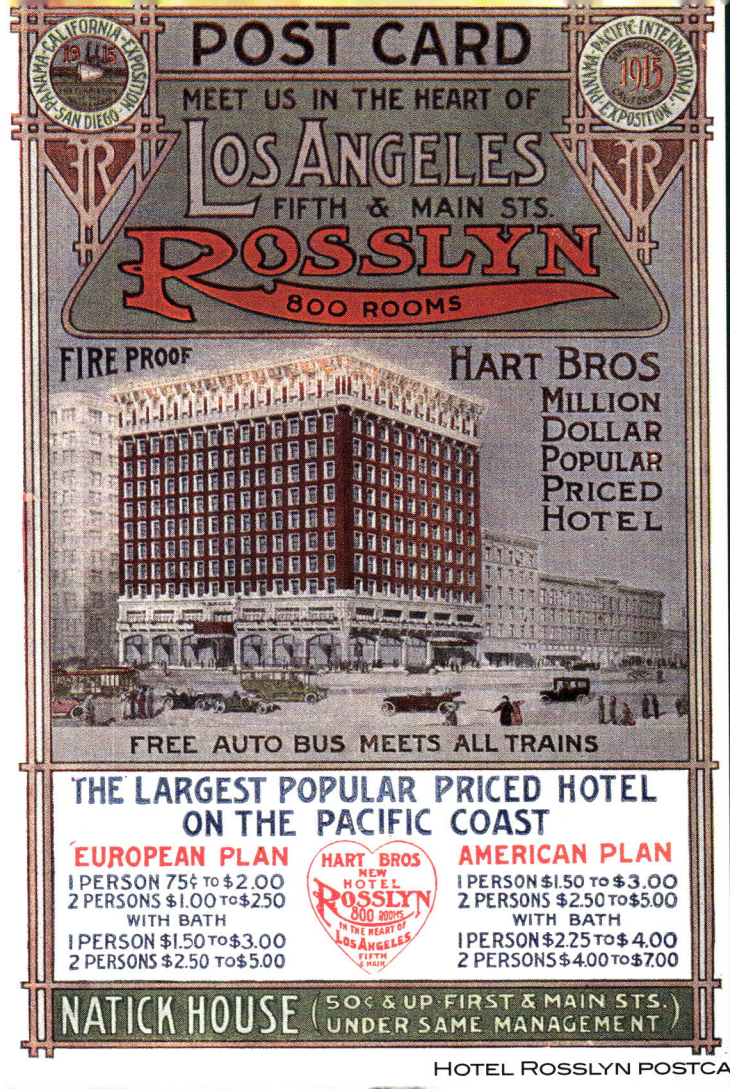

HOTEL ROSSLYN POSTCARD ADVERTISEMENT

CITIZEN'S NATIONAL BANK BUILDING

LOS ANGELES TRUST AND SAVINGS BANK

THE BROADWAY DEPARTMENT STORE

of Salt Lake City to anyone who will stop and consider its natural resources," Parkinson told the *Salt Lake Tribune* in 1909. "With such advantages as it possesses on every side and its location in regard to other cities, it must in the nature of things move forward constantly. As soon as the Thomas Kearns office building is started, we intend to establish a permanent office in Salt Lake City." Parkinson was so impressed with the business prospects in Salt Lake City that in July of 1909, he invested $41,400 of his own money in a plot on Main Street he intended to develop.

Parkinson & Bergstrom created plans for a steel, brick, and reinforced-concrete structure that would make an imposing statement on the downtown Salt Lake City skyline. When the Kearns Building was completed, its towering, unbroken piers divided by recessed paired windows, would invite comparisons to Louis Sullivan and Dankmar Adler's design for the Guaranty Building in Buffalo, New York. Kearns was so impressed with the design, he recommended the firm to the Church of Jesus Christ of Latter-day Saints, which, along with private investors, was planning to build a hotel on the corner of Main Street and South Temple.

And not just any hotel. Parkinson & Bergstrom had scored an opportunity to design one of the state's most significant buildings, the Hotel Utah. The road ahead was rough, however. Construction was disrupted twice by violent protests, but even the most aggressive opponents could not stop the creation of what Parkinson described as "the most perfectly arranged hotel in the United States."

Parkinson & Bergstrom were officially hired on May 26, 1909, and work on a ten-story Italian Renaissance hotel began the following month. The local firm of Raleigh and Harmon was used to excavate the ground, and the building contract was awarded to the St. Louis firm, James Black Masonry and Contracting Company, which had built the Washington Hotel in Seattle. The selection of the American Bridge Company of Chicago to provide 3,700 tons of steel, however, would prove problematic. The group was viewed as unfriendly to organized labor and frowned upon by the Chicago-based Industrial Workers of the World (IWW).

The IWW also found fault with the Jones Construction Company of San Francisco, which had been sub-contracted to erect the building's steel skeleton. Jones Construction hired both union and non-union labor and generally paid wages higher than union scale, but its presence alone was enough to rile a small group of pro-union supporters who ambushed construction boss Richard

Jones, attacking him with a knife as he made his way home one early-December evening. His brother-in-law Frank Carrick fired several shots and scared off the attackers, but worse events were to follow.

Three weeks later, saboteurs attempted to delay construction by using dynamite to blow up the hoisting engine and derrick at the building site, leaving an eight-foot crater in the ground. The equipment targeted was not significantly damaged and two men, Fred Wilson and John Delaney, were later apprehended and charged with the crime.

The following April, a second explosion was planned and timed to coincide with the rare sighting of Halley's Comet in the Utah sky. A bomb, left on the first floor of steel beams, exploded at three in the morning on April 18, shattering windows within a three-block radius and destroying the entrance of the nearby Utah State Bank. The explosion, which many residents wrongly believed was caused by the comet, twisted many of the hotel's giant steel beams and caused widespread panic. Although no arrests were made, local authorities were later tipped off that the bombers were closely linked to John J. and James B. McNamara, who bombed the Los Angeles Times building in October of 1910, an attack that claimed twenty-one lives.

Despite such violence, the construction of the Hotel Utah quickly resumed and as many as 550 workers were employed daily on the project. In addition to vast quantities of steel, 3.5 million bricks and twenty-five thousand barrels of cement were needed to bring Parkinson & Bergstrom's vision to life. The hotel's exterior would be finished with a pure white glazed terra cotta specifically brought in from Los Angeles.

Even with all of the delays, the Hotel Utah opened for business two months ahead of schedule. On June 9, 1911, the first guests walked through the hotel's entrance and cast their eyes upon the grandeur of the thirty-foot-high, eighty-seven-square-foot lobby surrounded by twelve grand marble pillars, each measuring four feet in diameter and providing the support for an exquisite art-glass ceiling. The hotel boasted three hundred ornately decorated guest rooms.

Just weeks after it opened, President William Howard Taft stayed in the Presidential Suite and declared the Hotel Utah to be, "a hotel that ranks with any in the world." The *New York Hotel Record* reported, "There are some larger in the great cities of this country, but the promoters declare there will be none finer in equipment, furnishings and general efficiency."

The following spring, a reporter from the *Los Angeles Times* was dispatched to the offices of Parkinson & Bergstrom and found the architects hard at work with more than four million dollars worth of

KEARNS BUILDING, SALT LAKE CITY

TITLE INSURANCE BUILDING

HOTEL UTAH, SALT LAKE CITY

HOTEL UTAH, LOBBY

HOTEL UTAH, MEZZANINE

G. EDWIN BERGSTROM RESIDENCE

new construction projects on the books, including the new twelve-story Rosslyn Hotel on Fifth and Main streets and a new factory for the Ford Motor Company. The *Times* marveled at the sheer number of structures Parkinson had designed since he first arrived in Los Angeles, a list that now included the Union Oil Building, Security Building, Los Angeles Athletic Club and O.T. Johnson Building, among others. By Parkinson's own calculation, the firm of Parkinson & Bergstrom was responsible for eighty percent of the modern office buildings in the city.

Despite their extraordinary success, the partnership of Parkinson & Bergstrom did not extend beyond the agreed-upon ten-year term. In 1915, John Parkinson and Edwin Bergstrom quietly went their separate ways. Parkinson reverted to doing business in his own name, and Bergstrom eventually established his own practice.

A year after the partnership with Parkinson ended, Bergstrom became president of the Los Angeles Housing Committee and played a central role in the drafting of state housing and building laws. In 1921, he formed the Allied Architects Association of Los Angeles with John Mitchell and served as president until 1933. He also spent two years as president of the Southern California Chapter of the American Institute of Architects. In 1939, he was elected president of the American Institute of Architects and was re-elected in 1940.

Over the years, Bergstrom would compete with his former partner for several high-profile projects, and although he would never match the volume of work produced by Parkinson's practice, he would design numerous significant structures in the region. George Edwin Bergstom's projects include the Pasadena Civic Auditorium (with John Bennett and Fitch Haskell), Grauman's Metropolitan Theater (with William Lee Woollett), and his most well-known endeavor, the Pentagon, home to the U.S. Department of Defense, in Arlington, Virginia.

In 1911, Parkinson reorganized Los Angeles's Central Park (now Pershing Square) by replacing winding pathways with twenty-foot-wide diagonal walks that intersected at a fountain. He considered the project to be his civic duty and donated his time.

TITLE INSURANCE BUILDING,
SECURITY BUILDING,
SECURITY NATIONAL BANK

WAR, TRADE AND EDUCATION

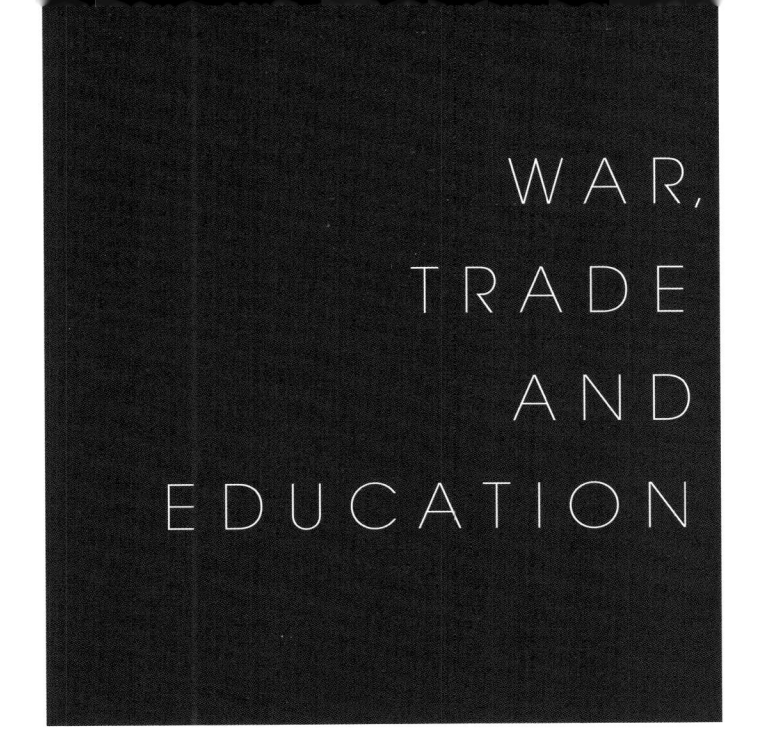

DONALD B. PARKINSON

THE SPECTER OF THE WORLD WAR 1 CAST A DARK SHADOW OVER THE WHOLE OF THE UNITED STATES. Two decades of relentless growth and optimism was gradually being overtaken by caution and fear as many Americans sensed the inevitability of their nation being drawn into an historic conflict. Although parts of the U.S. economy benefited from increased exports to Europe, numerous costly construction projects across the homeland were put on hold indefinitely. John Parkinson's architectural enterprise would be shielded from these uncertain times by one of the most ambitious building projects ever undertaken in Los Angeles, but it would not be long before the war hit close to home, impacting the lives of his own family and employees as well.

On the morning of December 16, 1916, Parkinson carried an enormous roll of architectural plans and walked into the office of Los Angeles Building Inspector J.J. Backus.

It was Parkinson's third visit to the city hall office in a week. Juggling multiple projects, he had previously delivered an application for $450,000 worth of construction for a new store for the N.B. Blackstone dry goods company and an eighty-thousand-dollar application for a new headquarters for the tea-and-coffee traders, Joannes Brothers Company. "I was fortunate to have that work on hand during that depressing period," Parkinson later wrote.

On this visit, the stakes couldn't have been higher. Parkinson was attempting to secure a building permit for the costliest construction project in the city's history. The proposed Los Angeles Wholesale Terminal Market had an estimated price tag of as high as ten million dollars. The two men smiled and posed for a photograph for the *Los Angeles Times* as Parkinson handed over his designs for $2.5 million worth of buildings, comprising the first phase of construction.

Planners had targeted a thirty-two acre site bounded by Seventh, Eighth and Alameda streets and Central Avenue as the location for the structure, the brainchild of Benjamin Johnson, president of the Los Angeles Public Market. Johnson, who had formed the market in 1907 with his brother Edward, envisioned the Wholesale Terminal Market as a modern way of eliminating the expense of moving produce between shipping terminals, warehouses, and markets by combining all of the facilities in one central location.

Johnson pitched the idea of a centralized market to Paul Shoup, president of the Pacific Electric Railway. Shoup understood the rail business from the ground up and saw the lucrative potential of locating a market and warehouses next to the company's freight facilities. He began his career in the mechanical department of the Santa Fe Railroad in San Bernardino, California. After learning telegraphy, he was hired as an operator with the Southern Pacific Railroad, where he rose rapidly through the ranks and was eventually put in charge of its subsidiary, the Pacific Electric Railway, a vast network of interurban and streetcar lines. "I learned to know Mr. Shoup well," Parkinson wrote. "He is one of the very big men of these United States."

Touting an exciting, big business opportunity—a brand new, single, central hub where the majority of all produce coming into Los Angeles would be handled—Shoup set about trying to attract investors.

The Los Angeles Union Terminal Company was formed and financed through the sale of $3.25 million in bonds to a syndicate

Security National Bank, detail

Security National Bank, interior

Security National Bank, columns

Security National Bank, glass ceiling

of Los Angeles and San Francisco businessmen. Parkinson's firm worked behind the scenes on planning a series of reinforced concrete structures for the Wholesale Terminal Market for two years before details were released to the press.

"It is planned to construct six buildings, each 1,250 feet long, with a frontage of a hundred feet on Seventh Street, four of which will be six stories high, and two to be used by the Los Angeles public market, two stories in height," the *Electric Railway Journal* reported. "These will be supplemented by a market yard 1,200 feet long and 180 feet wide. Each warehouse building is to have an eighty-foot private paved street on one side and separate tracks on the other." In the end, more than two miles of railway track would surround the terminal.

The *Los Angeles Examiner* called Parkinson's designs "the most elaborate and extensive ever delivered at City Hall." The initial permit application was for two six-story wholesale buildings and a pair of two-story buildings to house the public market. The *Los Angeles Times* reported the elevator order for the first phase of construction would be "the largest ever placed in the west."

In anticipation of the permit being approved, excavation work for the foundations got underway, and the entire area was cleared. The old Pacific Electric Railway car barns on the site were demolished, and new ones were constructed in Watts, Vineyard and Covina Junction. Even before the work began, half of the warehouse spaces had been leased, and the price of neighboring property skyrocketed.

Meanwhile, the Pacific Electric Railway entered into an agreement with the city to operate the municipally owned sections of the railway that linked to the Los Angeles harbor, and it was agreed all produce delivered to the terminal market would be subject to a switching charge. Critical of the operation, a Federal Trade Commission report on the wholesale marketing of food later declared, "...the terminal market as it stands is simply a land improvement speculation and a monopoly controlled by one railroad."

In April of 1917, the United States formally entered the First World War. At age fifty-five, Parkinson was, by his own admission, "too old for strenuous service," and instead joined prominent Los Angeles attorneys Henry O'Melveny and Jud R. Rush on a panel to evaluate potential officers for the army's engineering force. In all, eight employees of Parkinson's firm, as well as his son Donald, who was studying architecture at the Massachusetts Institute of Technology, would join the war effort. Only one employee, Captain Westcott, failed to return.

"My son enlisted to become an aviator and attended the ground school at Berkeley. [He] later was sent to March Field where he learned to fly," Parkinson remembered. "I took an interest in the San Diego Ship Building Company. We started a shipyard in San Diego, and for a time I was president of the company until the government required our plant and took it off our hands to build concrete ships. During my connection with this concern I acquired a slight knowledge of ship construction."

As the war in Europe raged on, Parkinson oversaw the massive construction of the Los Angeles Wholesale Terminal Market. It opened for business in 1918 and was described as "the best-appointed and most complete terminal market in the United States." Journalists marveled at the enormous cold-storage plant considered to be among the finest in the country. Almost all of the five hundred stalls in the open market were leased before a single customer stepped inside.

The complex was so large, the Los Angeles Trust and Savings Bank announced plans to open a "Wholesale Terminal Branch" and asked Parkinson to design it. The Western Union and

JOANNES BROS. CO. BUILDING

N.B. BLACKSTONE BUILDING

WAR, TRADE AND EDUCATION

ICONIC VISION

Los Angeles Wholesale Terminal Market

ADMINISTRATION
BUILDING, USC;
ORIGINAL DESIGN

EAST ELEVATION

ADMINISTRATION
BUILDING, USC

Postal Telegraph Companies also announced plans to follow suit, as did the Los Angeles Produce Exchange, the Walnut Growers' Association, the California Fruit Growers' Exchange, and the Agricultural Department's local Bureau of Markets. The complex also had a Japanese and a Chinese restaurant, and there was a hotel for farmers called the Inside Inn.

While previous markets in the city had been crowded with horses and buggies, the new Wholesale Terminal Market was designed to accommodate automobiles. A repair shop and a filling station were located inside the property to serve delivery trucks.

Every morning (excluding Sundays), trading began at three o'clock, and continued nonstop into the late evening. Although most of the produce would serve Southern California and nearby states, such as Nevada and Arizona, locally produced goods were now being shipped as far as Colorado, Utah, Washington, and even to the East Coast.

By the early 1940s, the bustling market was handling an estimated forty-five million dollars worth of fruits and vegetables, almost all the "fresh garden produce consumed in the city,

USC PRESIDENT GEORGE FINLEY BOVARD

ADMINISTRATION BUILDING, USC

WAR, TRADE AND EDUCATION 103

PHYSICAL EDUCATION
BUILDING, USC,
UNDER
CONSTRUCTION

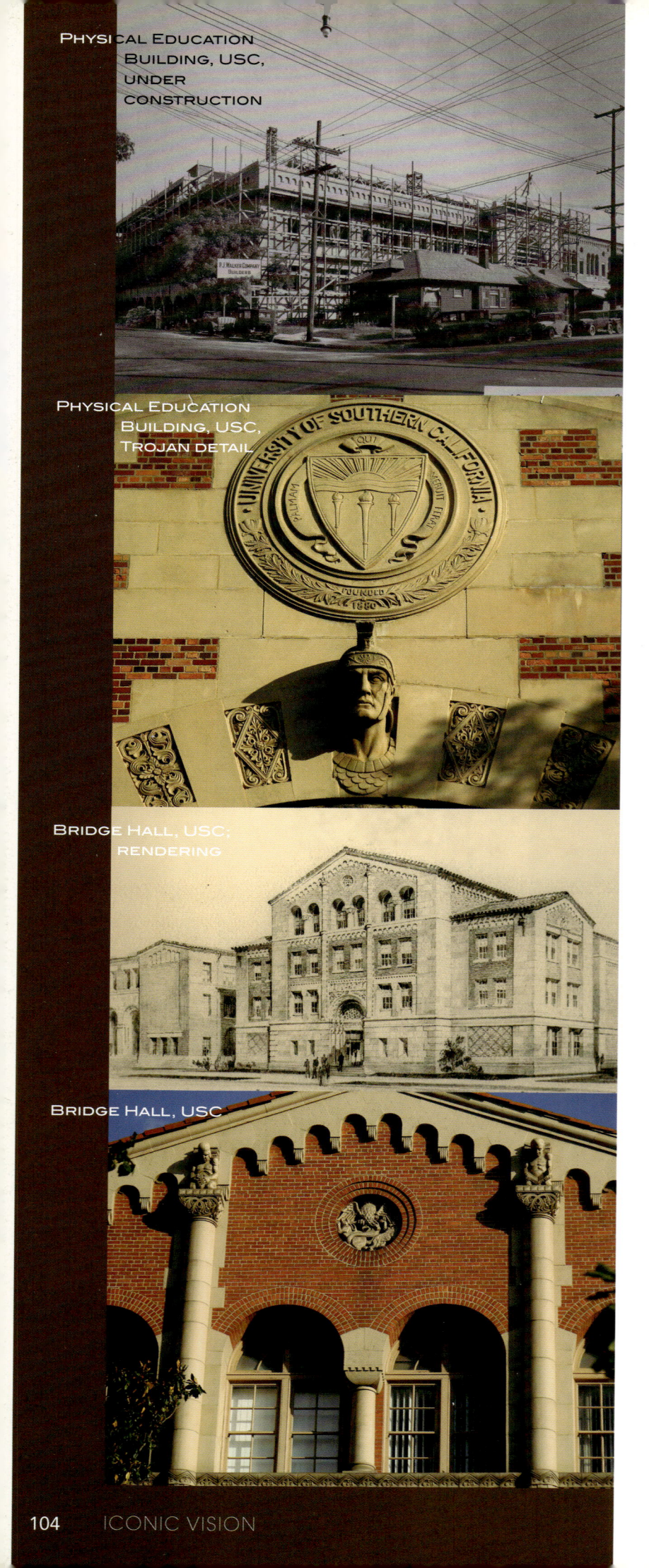

PHYSICAL EDUCATION
BUILDING, USC,
TROJAN DETAIL

BRIDGE HALL, USC;
RENDERING

BRIDGE HALL, USC

annually passes through it and the smaller markets nearby." The Wholesale Terminal Market remained home to the most important wholesale market in the city for nearly seventy years—until 1986, when a modern facility was constructed on the north side of Olympic Boulevard between Central Avenue and Alameda Street.

THE UNIVERSITY OF SOUTHERN CALIFORNIA

When the First World War ended in 1918 and confidence returned to the construction industry, Parkinson's firm was ready to take full advantage. One of his first post-war commissions was a master plan for the University of Southern California. In the spring of 1919, University President George Finley Bovard approached Parkinson to design the first in a series of structures that would set the university on a path to becoming one of the premier educational establishments in the nation.

Founded in 1879 as a Methodist institution, USC commenced on an eighteen-acre plot adjacent to what later became known as Exposition Park. The next year, the school's doors opened for the first time, welcoming ten teachers and fifty-three students. The population of Los Angeles as a whole in 1880 was 11,183. By 1919, nearly four decades later, it was approaching six hundred thousand, and the number of students on campus had grown to more than four thousand. Los Angeles had replaced San Francisco as the largest city on the West Coast, and President Bovard knew he needed a bold vision.

A former USC student, Bovard became the university's president in 1903. After resisting offers from real-estate developers to move the school, he embarked on a campaign to expand it. His efforts were disrupted by the onset of the First World War, but enough funds were available in 1919 for its board of trustees to authorize the construction of a new administration building on University Avenue between 35th Place and 36th Street.

John Parkinson was a coveted choice to design the structure since he was now, arguably, the most acclaimed architect in the region and, coincidentally, with an accomplished background designing educational facilities, including the nearby Manual Arts High School campus, as well as numerous schools during his time as the Seattle school board's staff architect.

In a departure from traditional campus design, Parkinson's plans called for a series of structures that could easily be accessed by automobile along University Avenue. He selected an Italian Romanesque style he felt best suited the Southern California climate and provided the greatest

In 1927, John and Donald Parkinson initially estimated the cost of the USC Student Union Building to be $350,000.

WAR, TRADE AND EDUCATION 105

USC STUDENT UNION
BUILDING, DETAILS

flexibility for future expansion when considering the varied purposes of the proposed buildings.

"The interesting thing about Parkinson's choice," historian Kenneth Breisch explains, "is that it was in contrast to northern European Gothic or East Coast universities like Yale or the University of Pennsylvania. He was looking to emulate the architecture of the great university of the Middle Ages. He felt probably that that wasn't an appropriate style for a Mediterranean setting as he envisioned Southern California. But it did of course reflect the great Italian law schools, theological schools, medieval universities that were contemporary with universities in Paris or Oxford and Cambridge."

On September 30, 1919, Parkinson met with city building inspector Backus to deliver a permit application for a new administration building that would be the focal point of the campus. The estimated cost of the building was a half-million dollars. As the *Los Angeles Times* reported that year, Parkinson's design called for a three-story, 260-square-foot structure with two wings separated by a thirty-seven-square-foot tower standing 116-feet high. The wings would be connected by large, open corridors, and the main entrance would be located at the front of the tower with several additional entrances located on either side.

As much as possible, all the materials used in construction would be manufactured in Southern California. The steel-frame and concrete structure would be faced with hard wire-cut brick in various colors that ranged from purple to brown, the *Times* detailed. A mixture of stone and terra cotta would be used for the trim, while the roof would be covered with a predominantly red mission tile.

It was agreed the university's executive offices would be located on the ground floor, and the second and third stories would house twenty-eight modern classrooms. Between the two wings, Parkinson designed a bowl-shaped auditorium, featuring a thirty-five-thousand-dollar organ boasting five thousand pipes. The ground floor would seat 1,078, while the two balconies each would seat five hundred. Local newspapers predicted the fifty-six-foot-long stage would vie with those of downtown theaters in size and equipment.

In October, Parkinson attended a simple groundbreaking ceremony where he joined William M. Bowen of the board of trustees; Dr. Thomas B. Stowell, dean emeritus of the school of education; Claude Reeves, president of the student body; and

President Bovard who turned the first shovel of earth. Expectations were that the building would be finished in fifteen months. Soon afterwards, the cornerstone was laid, and placed inside were university and Methodist documents, local newspapers, and other items representing life in 1919, including a picture of President Woodrow Wilson and his cabinet, and the 1919 USC yearbook.

In 1920, President Bovard announced a new five-million-dollar-fundraising campaign, with half the money intended for construction of new buildings and the other half as an endowment. The campaign was launched with a twenty-five thousand dollar donation from Edward L. Doheny, Jr., son of the Los Angeles oil baron. "We are faced by the fact that we either must either enlarge our plant in order that we may adequately serve those who come to us for accommodations, or, in the very near future, refuse to admit hundreds of new students," Bovard told the *Los Angeles Times*. "Last year we had a total enrollment of 4,375 students, and the registration for this year promises to exceed that of last year."

In the spring of 1921, President Bovard announced he would be stepping down due to poor health and instructed the university's trustees to begin the search for a new president. In recognition of his service to the school, the university's trustees voted to officially name the administration building the Bovard Administration Building, and the completed structure was formally dedicated June 19-23, 1921.

In October of that year, President Rufus Bernhard Von KleinSmid of the University of Arizona was recruited to replace Bovard. Upon his inauguration in April of 1922, the university had 5,635 students and was made up of eight schools and colleges, making USC the second-largest educational institution in California.

Von KleinSmid soon began an ambitious drive to raise ten million dollars to help the university keep pace with growing enrollment. Although he failed to reach the lofty target, a series of new buildings were erected. The Parkinson firm would design twenty projects for USC, although many were never realized. Soon after Von KleinSmid took office, the Parkinson firm began work on plans for the Science Building (1923), followed by the Law School (1925), Bridge Hall (1927) the Physical Education Building (1930) and Town & Gown Foyer (1935). As the campus expanded, perimeter walls were built and University Way became a pedestrian center. Today, eight Parkinson-designed structures remain and continue to be an integral part of daily life on the campus.

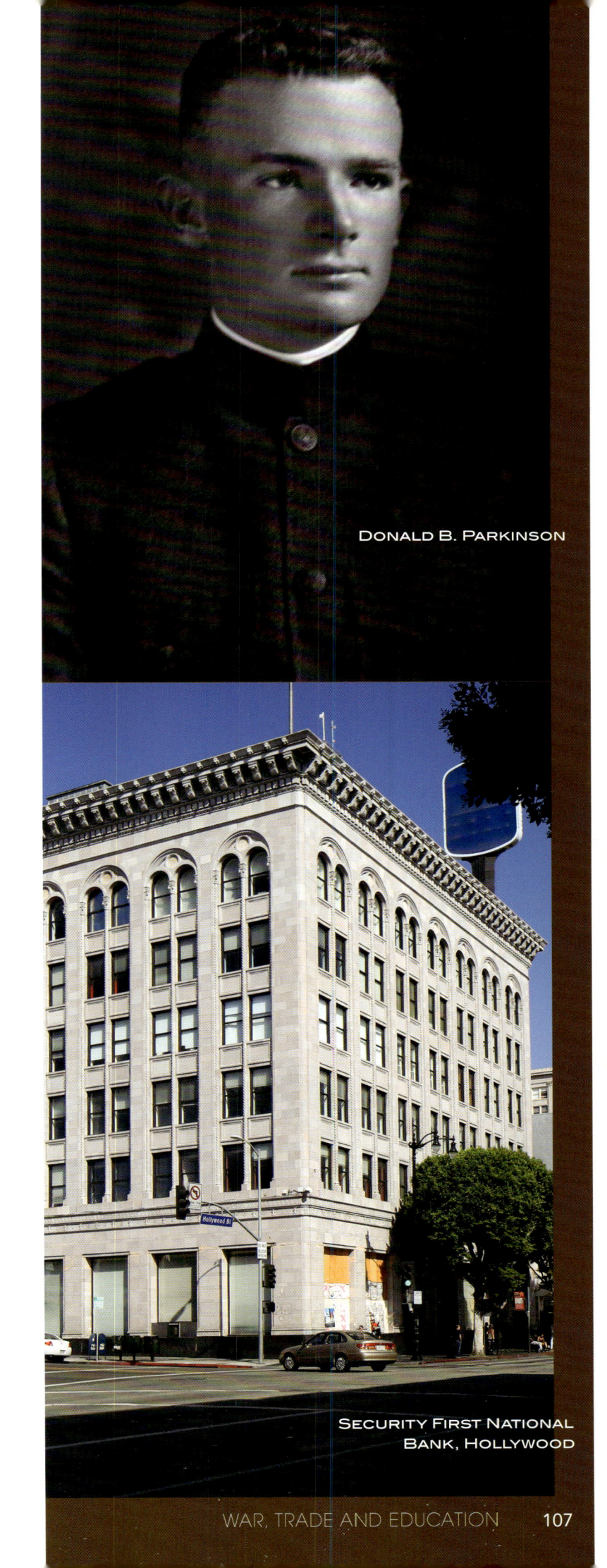

DONALD B. PARKINSON

SECURITY FIRST NATIONAL BANK, HOLLYWOOD

WAR, TRADE AND EDUCATION

Donald B. Parkinson

JOHN & DONALD PARKINSON

JOHN AND DONALD PARKINSON

NOW THE MOST RESPECTED ARCHITECT IN LOS ANGELES, JOHN PARKINSON DID NOT NEED A NEW BUSINESS PARTNER TO ENHANCE HIS CREDENTIALS, BUT ONE INDIVIDUAL DID MANAGE TO CAPTURE PARKINSON'S ATTENTION—HIS OWN SON, DONALD. The creative passion Donald offered energized his father's practice, and together they formed a remarkable alliance that shaped many of the city's most beloved landmarks.

Donald Berthold Parkinson, his father joked, was "educated with difficulty in the Los Angeles Public Schools." In 1914, he enrolled in the Massachusetts Institute of Technology School of Architecture. Although his education was interrupted by his service during the First World War, he graduated from MIT in 1920 and spent a year as a special student at the American Academy in Rome before returning to Los Angeles.

An extraordinarily gifted artist, Donald also had a reputation as a daredevil and a risk taker. "He was extremely intelligent, he was hard working, but he played hard, he drank too much, [and] he drove too fast. He could be wild," his granddaughter Pamela Parkinson Kellogg explains. In the fall of 1921, Donald married sculptor Frances Grace Wells, daughter of Ralph Evans Wells, general manager of the San Pedro, Los Angeles and Salt Lake Railroad. For their honeymoon, the couple spent six months looking for artistic inspiration on a European road trip.

When Donald returned to Los Angeles, he found his father hard at work on plans for the Los Angeles Memorial Coliseum, a seventy-five-thousand-capacity stadium that would play a central role in an audacious bid to bring the Olympic Games to the city. John Parkinson was so impressed by his son's potential, he quickly made him a partner and going forward, the firm would conduct business as John and Donald B. Parkinson Architects. "They make a splendid team, one with his ripe experience, and the other with the enthusiasm of youth," John C. Austin later wrote.

As the duo settled into their new partnership, they drew plans for their own personal homes located in Santa Monica, less than a half-mile from the Pacific Ocean. The *Architectural Forum* reported that John Parkinson's house had "real distinction and dignity," and compared the design to a Tuscan villa due to its central structures and projecting wings. The triple arches of the entrance loggia dominated the front of the property.

Nearby, Donald's single-story Spanish Colonial Revival-style residence, reached by way of a winding, cypress-lined driveway, was dominated by a series of arched windows that later drew comparisons to those installed at the Parkinson-designed landmark, Union Station. The home featured a red tile roof and garden courtyards, as well as an art studio for his wife, and a series of garages to store Donald's exotic sports car collection.

Both architects could easily afford expensive properties as business was booming. In the coming months, father and son would begin work on a host of new projects, including a collaboration with John C. Austin on a new two-million-dollar Chamber of Commerce Building on Twelfth and Hill streets, and a new six-hundred-thousand-dollar school project located on the corner of Fairfax and Melrose avenues.

Although the elder Parkinson enjoyed a revered status

PARKINSON DESIGN FOR CENTRAL PARK BEACON; UNBUILT

JOHN PARKINSON AND FLORENCE GUMAER

among Los Angeles architects, he didn't always get his own way. Upon learning the Board of Library Directors planned to appoint an architect for a new two-million-dollar public library instead of holding an open competition, Parkinson considered his legal options. Library officials claimed negotiating directly with an architect would save time and expense, which infuriated Parkinson, who urged members of the Public Welfare Committee of the City Council to block the library board's action. Although he was ultimately unsuccessful, and the work given to East Coast architect Bertram G. Goodhue, losing out on such an important contract was rare for Parkinson.

A PRIVATE TRAGEDY

As John Parkinson's professional career reached new highs, his private life was about to hit a desperate low. On March 6, 1922, his wife Meta became sick and was confined to bed. Dr. F.J. Wagner was called to the Parkinson family's Santa Monica home where Meta was diagnosed as suffering from throat and ear streptococci infection. Four days later at 7:15 in the evening, Meta died from myocarditis at the age of fifty-nine. On March 13, at ten o'clock in the morning, funeral services were conducted at the St. James Episcopal Church, officiated by Reverend Ray. O. Miller. Cremation followed at the Los Angeles Crematory.

It was a devastating loss for the Parkinsons. Donald no longer had his mother, and his grieving father had lost his longtime partner of more than thirty years, the woman who had stood by him from his early days in Napa, his successes and failures in Seattle, and his early struggles in Los Angeles.

The months passed, and as Parkinson attempted to move on with his life, he struck up a friendship with a charming bank teller, Florence Gumaer, who worked at the Bank of Santa Monica. Although Parkinson was twenty-three years her senior, they quickly discovered a romantic connection. Born in 1884 in Buffalo, New York, Gumaer's mother died when she was four-years-old. Her father Adelbert George Gumaer, a physician from Alabama, New York, remarried two years later. When he died in the summer of 1909, her grandmother took over responsibility for her care.

After a brief courtship, the couple married in Pasadena on April 4, 1923. As Gumaer's niece Melissa McCollister remembered, they made a good partnership. "He was definitely the love of her life, and although she was thirty-eight, she was waiting for this man to come along and probably sweep her off her feet. My aunt was

110 ICONIC VISION

Fairfax High School

Los Angeles Gas and
Electric Building

112 ICONIC VISION

WOODACRES, JOHN PARKINSON RESIDENCE, SANTA MONICA

always a mature person. The age difference was not a problem at all."

Other family members, including Parkinson's daughter-in-law Grace, did not always share his enthusiasm for the marriage. "My grandmother placed way too much emphasis on social class and family background and would have been a lot more comfortable if JP had married someone from a proper—in the view of my grandmother—Los Angeles family," Pamela Parkinson Kellogg explains. "For JP's children, Dorothea and Donald, it may have been very hard because she wasn't that much older than they were. That being said, she was a delightful woman. I have memories of her being so warm and interested in us as children. It's hard to imagine her not winning over everyone in time."

A TIME TO EXPERIMENT

John Parkinson's passion for incorporating the latest architectural techniques into his work was equally shared by his son, and the Roaring Twenties welcomed such bold expression. During the postwar years from 1920 to 1930, Los Angeles grew at a phenomenal rate; its population more than doubled from 576,000 to 1,238,000. It was an exciting era full of growth and possibility and a unique opportunity for the city's leading architects who embraced a myriad of new innovative design forms.

As Los Angeles' downtown business core expanded, John and Donald Parkinson created numerous cutting-edge structures that reflected their creative innovation and spoke to an age of prosperity.

The father-and-son team freely experimented with what would become known as Art Deco in their plans for the Title Insurance Building and the Banks Huntley Building on Spring Street and the Title Guarantee Building on the corner of South Hill and West 5th streets. In the mid 1920s, the firm's most celebrated artistic expression of the period culminated in the creation of a masterpiece, Bullock's Wilshire. Located outside of the downtown corridor, the luxurious specialty store set a whole new standard for the incorporation of modern art into building design, while also reflecting Los Angeles' growing automobile culture.

After the Title Insurance Building was completed, John and Donald Parkinson relocated their offices inside. The two-million-dollar structure designed for the Title Insurance and Trust Company, the leading title and insurance company in Southern California, was later nicknamed, "the Queen of Spring Street." The exterior terra cotta displayed a travertine-like finish, complemented inside by real travertine and marble in the public areas. Artist Herman Sachs was recruited to decorate the lobby ceiling and Hugo Ballin to create the tile murals above the street entrance.

Here, John and Donald Parkinson masterminded the completion of their greatest architectural achievement, the new Los Angeles City Hall. Architects from across the United States submitted bids for the prestigious commission, but the team of John Parkinson, John C. Austin, and Albert C. Martin emerged victorious. The path ahead of them, however, was long and laden with obstacles. John and Donald Parkinson were responsible for the overall design, and the much-anticipated completion of the five-million-dollar structure in 1928 capped a difficult, drawn-out chapter in local politics.

Amidst all the fanfare and excitement surrounding the creation of City Hall, John Parkinson soon had another reason to celebrate. On December 16, 1926, Donald and his wife, Grace,

Title Insurance Building; rendering

welcomed their first child, a son, Donald Wells Parkinson. Days later, John Parkinson penned the following in a letter to Grace:

"Dear Grace, Thanks for the fine boy—may he live long and be worthy in the future of being remembered for his talents and for his services to his country and to mankind, may he love nature, art and beautiful things have a strong body and good health, may he appreciate everything to the full the creator has so bountifully and perfectly provided for his mind and body, and may you and Don live to see him grow up and develop for many, many years, affectionately, JP."

To his son, Donald, Parkinson reflected on his joy over the success of their partnership:

"Dear Don, a Merry Christmas and I want to add that it is a great joy true the way you are developing and also the way that you are taking hold of the office work. The great thing is to do things well, and develop the best that can be done, real art, sound construction and practical and effective. These are the real results desired, the business should pay in order to exist and progress, but great profits are secondary to good work. I forgot to tell Grace that as soon as you decide upon the boy's name I will start an account for him of $500. Please tell her. Affectionately, Dad."

While Donald Parkinson's life appeared settled, his sister, Dorothea, and her husband, Goodwin M. Trent, would soon experience a life altering tragedy. On June 13, 1927, their two-and-a-half year old daughter, Christine, drowned after she fell into a reservoir on the Trent Ranch near San Marcos. She managed to climb a wall surrounding the reservoir before falling in. Hearing the screams from her child's playmates, Dorothea rushed to the scene and plunged in, as did her mother-in-law, Mary Delorme Trent. Dorothea pulled her daughter out of the water but was unable to save her. Mrs. Trent, who could not swim, likely would have drowned too, had her son not arrived in time to rescue her. Emergency services were called in to help revive Christine, but it was too late.

John Parkinson dealt with the loss of his granddaughter by focusing much of his attention on his work. In 1927, the Parkinsons' architectural firm oversaw the construction of the Spreckels Building on the corner of Sixth and Broadway in San Diego. The two-million-dollar, thirteen-story structure took two years to build, and when

TITLE INSURANCE BUILDING, EXTERIOR

TITLE INSURANCE BUILDING, DETAIL

TITLE INSURANCE BUILDING, EXTERIOR

DONALD WELLS PARKINSON AND HIS MOTHER GRACE

TITLE GUARANTEE BUILDING

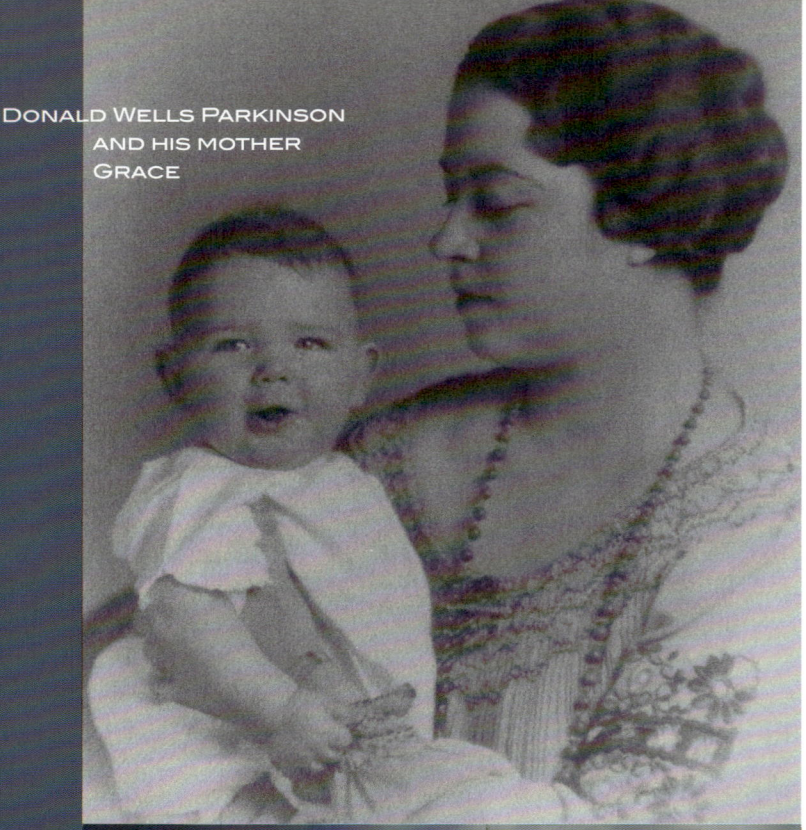

completed, was the tallest building in the city.

Soon afterwards, they began work on plans for the Southern California Telephone Company Building on Olive Street in Los Angeles and were hired as consulting architects to work with architect Samuel Lunden on the Los Angeles Stock Exchange on Spring Street. The moderne design they chose was intended to emphasize security and stability. The walls of the lobbies and stairways were covered in sienna travertine and featured the latest in modern lighting and sound proofing. The boardroom was reported to be the largest outside of New York City. By the time the $1.65 million structure opened for business, the Great Depression had cast a dark shadow over the construction industry and the country as a whole.

THE DEATH OF AN ICON

Although Los Angeles was hit hard by the Depression of the 1930s, John and Donald Parkinson's practice survived with a series of high-profile commissions that showcased their mastery of Streamline and Classical Moderne design.

In 1930, construction began on the Federal Reserve Bank of San Francisco Los Angeles Branch. It was one of the first Classical Moderne structures in the city. The architectural style, popular during the Depression years for government and financial institutions, represented a significant transition for the firm of John and Donald Parkinson who later received an AIA Honor Award for their efforts.

The building featured a California gray granite façade with matching terra cotta and was decorated with an ornate bronze grillwork and spandrel panels. Some 1,600 tons of steel were used to build the structure's skeleton. Artist Edgar Walter was hired to create the relief sculpture above the entrance. The total cost of contruction was $1,284,900.

At the same time, John and Donald Parkinson would see their work come to life in plans for the E.F. Hutton Building on Spring Street and the California Bank on Hollywood Boulevard.

The Parkinsons' practice was busier than ever, but John Parkinson's contributions to Los Angeles would soon come to an unexpected end. In the midst of working on designs for the Los Angeles Union Passenger Terminal, which came to be known as Union Station, he suffered what was later diagnosed as a mild heart attack while working at his office in the Title Insurance Building.

He remained at his Santa Monica home to recuperate. On December 9, 1935, Dr. C.E. Rooney paid Parkinson a visit and found

116 ICONIC VISION

The Parkinson-designed California Club on 5th and Hill Streets was demolished to make way for the Title Guarantee Building

FEDERAL RESERVE BANK OF SAN FRANCISCO,
LOS ANGELES BRANCH, UNDER
CONSTRUCTION

him to be "cheerful and happy." But a mere ten minutes after he left, the doctor was urgently summoned back to the house where he found Parkinson dead from a heart attack. It was three days before what would have been his seventy-fourth birthday.

The following morning, private funeral services were conducted at Parkinson's home, in the presence of his widow, his children, and a small group of close family friends, by Reverend Wallace Pierson of Santa Monica's St. Augustine-by-the Sea Episcopal Church. Afterwards, his body was entombed in the mausoleum at Forest Lawn Memorial Park in Glendale.

For Florence Parkinson, the architect's widow, the loss was overwhelming. "It was as if a light had gone out for her," her niece Melissa McCollister remembers. "Her life changed a lot after Uncle John died. She lost her best friend, her very best friend. Anyone could tell she was a little bit lonely."

News of John Parkinson's death featured prominently on the front page of most Los Angeles newspapers. "Career Ended Parkinson Rites Said" was the headline in the *Los Angeles Times*. The newspaper described Parkinson as the "dean of Southland architects" and in a later obituary compared him to the architects who designed the Strasbourg Cathedral or the Taj Mahal. "In this illustrious company of builders Los Angeles architect John Parkinson has earned a distinction that death can not obliterate," the reporter noted. "The passing years will bring ever added proof of how much the city owes to his vision and his artistry. In a modern age of business and industry he has won a reputation as one of America's foremost business architects and designers."

The Los Angeles Evening Herald & Express proclaimed, "His farsighted perspective, his love for beauty, and his ability to modernize in building had won worldwide renown for Mr. Parkinson." *The Illustrated Daily News* added, "His genius is perpetuated in the buildings in the city in which he made his home.". Equally flattering tributes also appeared in many architectural publications.

DONALD PARKINSON TAKES CONTROL

At the time of John Parkinson's death in late 1935, he and Donald had together designed more than two hundred buildings, and the firm was responsible for upwards of four hundred, representing a considerable collection of work, conservatively estimated at more than $150 million dollars in construction.

His remarkable legacy would prove to be both a powerful asset but an enormous burden as well. His son, Donald, readily

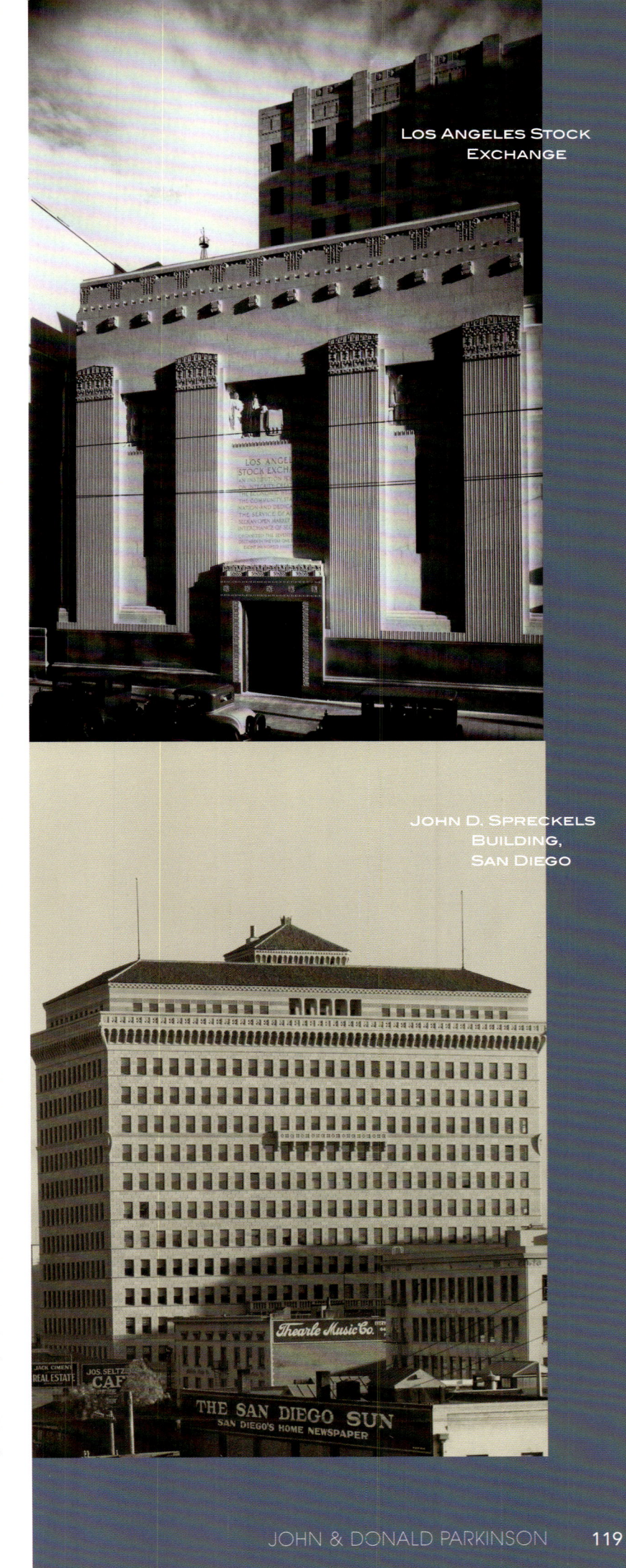

LOS ANGELES STOCK EXCHANGE

JOHN D. SPRECKELS BUILDING, SAN DIEGO

FEDERAL RESERVE
BANK OF SAN
FRANCISCO,
LOS ANGELES
BRANCH

assumed control of the business and continued to operate as John and Donald B. Parkinson out of respect for his father. His time at the helm would be cut short, however, by the onset of another world war and his own untimely death.

Donald began his career, certainly, in his father's shadow, but by virtue of his own tremendous talent, he established himself as one of the most accomplished architects of the day. In recognition of his artistic contributions to Los Angeles, he received five honor awards from the American Institute of Architects along with two certificates of merit. In 1940 he received an honorary mention in the 5th Pan American Congress of Architects, held in Montevideo, and the highest award from the Architectural Forum jury in the same year.

After taking the reigns of the most respected architectural firm in Los Angeles, Parkinson secured a series of important contracts and breathed new life into buildings originally designed by his father. His time in charge began by overseeing the completion of the Los Angeles Manual Arts High School. The original campus, designed by Parkinson & Bergstrom, was demolished after suffering extensive damage in the devastating 1933 earthquake. With limited funds at their disposal, the firm of John and Donald B. Parkinson created a series of two-story Streamline Moderne, reinforced-concrete structures, heralded nationwide as a model for low-cost school design. The Science Building and the Administration and Arts Building were the first to be erected and, like the structures that followed, featured distinct horizontal banding and rounded corners.

Although he respected his father's work, Donald Parkinson was not afraid to radically reinvent it, as he demonstrated in 1936 when the firm was hired to transform the Pacific Mutual Insurance Building on Sixth and Olive streets. Designed by Parkinson & Bergstrom in 1908, the office block resembled a Corinthian temple until Parkinson stepped in and added an Art Deco terra cotta exterior, rendering the original structure unrecognizable.

Outside of his architectural achievements, Donald Parkinson's love of modern technology, fast cars and airplanes led to a close friendship with Hollywood stunt pilot, Paul Mantz, and his frequent companion, Amelia Earhart. Donald Parkinson designed houses for both of them and even spent time as secretary and a director of Paul Mantz Air Services, a flight-instruction enterprise. He also served as a director for Bowlus Sailplanes, alongside aircraft-manufacturing titan Donald W. Douglas.

By 1940, with war being waged overseas, the U.S. Defense Department was looking for high-speed construction when Parkinson began work on the design for a state-of-the-art aircraft-manufacturing facility in Burbank, California. As Europe suffered through the Second World War, Parkinson's staff labored on plans for a seven-million-dollar plant for the Vega Airplane Company, a subsidiary of the Lockheed Aircraft Corpororation, that would play an important role in the Allies' victory plans.

The objective was to produce two thousand twin-engine bombers a year inside a vast complex of structures with more than a million square feet of floor space. Parkinson's design would allow a continuous flow of production from "rough stock to brake testing." The architect's draftsmen accommodated monorail conveyors, traveling bridge cranes and lifts connecting the shop floor with storage facilities. The main hub of activity was an enormous factory that stretched 850 by 600 feet, large enough to accommodate sixteen plane production lines running the length of the building.

Parkinson's firm designed fourteen structures, including a modern air-conditioned administration office facing the Lockheed Air Terminal, two engineering units, a fabrication, assembly and conveyor unit, as well as warehouse and underground storage. All of the buildings were fitted with the latest fluorescent lighting, with a record 36,524 tubes and 10,392 fixtures installed, allowing for twenty-four-hour production. Additionally, the property was protected by "one of the world's most complete sprinkler and anti-

Sculptor Edgar Walter created the panels above the main entrance to the Federal Reserve Bank of San Francisco, Los Angeles Branch

Banks Huntley Building

JOHN & DONALD PARKINSON

LOCKHEED, BURBANK

sabotage systems." Courtlandt S. Gross, president of the Vega Airplane Company was so pleased with Parkinson's work, he asked him to design his home in Bakersfield, California.

Parkinson eventually found himself juggling his architectural responsibilities with his own national service. In 1943, he re-enlisted as a major in the U.S. Army Corps of Engineers and was stationed in Phoenix, before being transferred closer to home to Culver City, California. The following year, he retired from active service and focused his considerable skill on the design of a $3.5 million modification base near the Lockheed Aircraft Corporation plant in Burbank. The new Navy Lockheed Service Center would occupy a seventy-seven-acre site and include two 160 by 400 feet hangars to house more than 1,500 workers.

In order to adhere to tight production deadlines, aircraft companies encouraged workers to eat on site in subsidized canteens. Taking it a big step further, in February of 1944, the Lockheed plant opened the doors to its new Parkinson-designed Employees Recreation Club Commissary, billed as the largest "hot food on the job" operation in the country.

Built at a cost of five hundred thousand dollars, the eatery covered an entire city block and was equipped to serve more than sixty thousand meals a day, six days a week. The main cafeteria was capable of serving 1,700 meals at a time and 24,000 meals every twenty-four hours. Reinforced-concrete columns and beams supported exterior walls of reinforced brick and a concrete-slab roof. The interior partitions were terra cotta tile.

As the war effort kept up on the homefront, Donald's son enlisted at Fort MacArthur in San Pedro, California, on June 16, 1945 as a private in the Air Corps, two months before the war came to an end. Five months later on the afternoon of November 17, 1945, Donald Parkinson died of a heart attack at his Santa Monica home. He was fifty years old. Services were conducted three days later at St Augustine by-the-Sea, and he was entombed near his father at the Forest Lawn Memorial Park in Glendale.

A DIFFICULT DECISION

Donald Wells Parkinson, known as Donny, shared his father's love of exotic cars, but he did not share the same bloodline passion for architecture. An only child, he studied to take over the Parkinson enterprise but struggled under the enormous weight of expectation placed upon him by the family.

His university education was surrounded by the legacy of his father and grandfather's lasting work. He enrolled as a student of architecture at the University of Southern California, where he was reminded daily of the extraordinary impact his family had made on the Los Angeles skyline. Donny Parkinson worked regularly at the offices of the family firm, but it was clear he derived more pleasure driving fast cars than designing buildings. As his daughter Pamela Parkinson Kellogg explains, "that put him at odds with the family, creating an increasingly difficult decision for him."

Growing up in Santa Monica, Parkinson became good friends with a young automobile enthusiast named Phil Hill who, one day, would go on to become the first American to win the Formula One World Driver's Championship. According to Parkinson Kellogg, the young Hill's hero and "the hero of many boys in the neighborhood was Donald Parkinson, who owned the coolest, fastest, most unusual cars, and Phil began sneaking over and checking out his cars."

Over time, Hill and the younger Parkinson became close

California Bank, Hollywood

John & Donald Parkinson

friends and racing rivals as they got older, and officially became family when Parkinson married Hill's sister, fellow USC student, Helen Naomi Hill, in a surprise wedding at Lake Arrowhead in the summer of 1949.

As he matured into an exciting, well-respected race-car driver, Parkinson invested in a high-priced Jaguar XK-120 purchased from Jaguar's Hollywood dealership, International Motors. He finished in second place behind Hill at Pebble Beach in November of 1950 and returned to the same course the following year determined to win the race. During a high-speed turn, however, his car rolled off the course, but Parkinson survived. He rebuilt his car, and in October of the same year, he raced to victory in the third Palm Springs Road Race. He invested in a new Jaguar C-type and returned to Pebble Beach, only to crash at the exact same corner..

In 1955, Parkinson decided to retire from racing, and he faced the burdensome choice of whether or not to follow in the gigantic footsteps of his father and grandfather. After struggling with depression for some time and facing difficult personal trials, Donny Parkinson committed suicide in October of 1955.

THE PARKINSON LEGACY

After Donald Parkinson's death in 1945, the architecture firm became known as Parkinson, Powelson, Briney, Bernard & Woodford. In 1956, it was renamed Woodford & Bernard and earned a reputation for specializing in communication and transportation projects. A decade later, John Parkinson's second wife, Florence, died after a long battle with Parkinson's disease. Even after she moved into a full-care facility in Pasadena, she insisted on returning regularly to the family's Woodacres home in Santa Monica to relive the memories of her life with John.

"She loved the house so much she couldn't let go of it," recalls McCollister. "And finally when she knew it was time to let go, she called me, I went down to visit her, and that was the last time I saw her. I could tell it was painful because she knew that this would be probably the last time she would be there among all the things that they had gathered together in their travels. Most of the house was furnished by them as a couple."

After Donald Parkinson died, his wife, Grace, continued to live in the Santa Monica house designed by her husband and later

MANUAL ARTS HIGH SCHOOL

remarried. Her passion for sculpture and the arts stayed with her until her death in September 1981.

In 1984, the same year the Olympics returned to the Coliseum, the Parkinson name was restored to the firm he created when Woodford & Bernard became known as Woodford, Parkinson, Wynn & Partners. In 1990, the Arizona-based DWL Architects acquired the firm and re-named their California operation DWL Parkinson Architects. In 1992, architect Scott Field became the sole owner of the firm, which he renamed Parkinson Field Associates. Field continues to maintain and care for the Parkinson Archives and has restored numerous Parkinson-designed structures while also working on original projects for the firm.

More than fifty Parkinson structures remain in downtown Los Angeles. Decades after it was constructed, Los Angeles City Hall is still the main seat of political power. The Coliseum, home to the USC Trojans, maintains its long-held reputation as the most historic sporting venue in Los Angeles and the only structure to have staged two Olympic Games. The Homer Laughlin Building continues as the home of the bustling Grand Central Market. And thousands of downtown-Los Angeles residents live in refurbished Parkinson-designed buildings, once home to busy offices generations ago and now converted into modern loft apartments for urbanites.

Bullock's Wilshire remains one of the most masterfully crafted structures ever conceived in the city and is enjoyed every day by the students and faculty of the Southwestern Law School. The administration building at USC is still the most recognizable structure at the university. And nearly seventy-five years after the first train arrived, bustling Union Station remains one of the city's most beloved architectural icons.

In these and numerous other structures, John Parkinson's legacy lives on.

His name may not be familiar to many Los Angeles citizens, yet John Parkinson and Los Angeles are forever entwined. His work can be seen in many places throughout the heart of the city, and as the decades pass, they remain an important, vibrant part of life in Los Angeles. More than any other architect, John Parkinson helped define the look and feel of Los Angeles as a city looking to the future. To gaze upon a Parkinson building is to feel the optimism of his time, a sense of hope that still speaks to us today

DONALD B. PARKINSON, IN WORLD WAR II UNIFORM

DONALD W. PARKINSON, IN WORLD WAR II UNIFORM

DONALD PARKINSON JOINED FORCES WITH JOSEPH M. ESTEP TO DESIGN SANTA MONICA CITY HALL.

200 CITY HALL

LOS ANGELES MEMORIAL COLISEUM

PARKINSON
ICONS

Los Angeles Memorial Coliseum, under construction

"I DOUBT IF ANY OTHER FIRM OF WESTERN ARCHITECTS HAS SUCH A RECORD OF BUILDINGS STANDING AND BUILT SINCE I LANDED IN SEATTLE THAT GREY, WET DAY IN JANUARY 1889."

—John Parkinson

THE "WORLD'S MIGHTIEST ATHLETIC DRAMA"

Los Angeles city leaders knew there was no more glorious prize to herald the city's arrival on the international stage than capturing the world's biggest athletic event, the Olympic Games.

On July 30, 1932, the dreams of an ambitious city were realized when 101,022 people crammed into the Los Angeles Memorial Coliseum, temporarily renamed Olympic Stadium, for the opening ceremony of the Xth Olympiad of the modern era. It was the largest crowd in Olympic history.

John Parkinson, who designed the mammoth structure, joined the sold-out crowd, which included visiting royalty, senators, congressmen, and tourists from across the globe. In the days leading up to the Games, a steady stream of automobiles, steamships, and airplanes transported tens of thousands of spectators to Los Angeles for what Vice President Charles Curtis confidently predicted would be "the greatest of all Olympiads." Even in the midst of a worldwide depression, the city's hotel lobbies were "jammed with excited crowds" and streets were "choked with hundreds of thousands of visitors," as the July 29, 1932, edition of the Los Angeles Examiner declared. More than 1.5 million people were expected to witness the Games or some part of them before they closed. All eyes now were on Los Angeles, only the second city in the United States to have hosted this epic event.

Just before three o'clock in the afternoon, the Parade of Nations, made up of 1,503 athletes from around the world, entered the sunlit amphitheater, smiling and waving to a jubilant crowd before forming military-style lines on the field. Reporter Arthur Bern summed up the excitement, "As the gleaming trumpets pealed the national anthem, for a moment in time you forgot the Depression, the rout of the Bonus Army three days ago, the terror of the war in Manchuria, Hitler's gains in the German election and all such weary cares. You remembered only that you loved your country, and that she stood for those splendid things typified by the nobility of the statuesque athletes assembled on the green grass under a sparkling sun."

Vice President Curtis stepped to the podium and declared the Games officially open. Ten cannons roared an Olympic formal salute before the Olympic torch burst into flames. An enormous choir sang the Olympic hymn as the Olympic flag slowly rose above the Peristyle Memorial Court of Honor. Two thousand racing pigeons were released before the official dedication and benediction, followed by flag bearers from each of the participating countries forming a semi-circle in front of the Tribune of Honor, where dignitaries and members of the Olympic Committee were seated.

Athletes from forty nations competed in 124 events in twenty-three sports. By the time the Games were over, sixteen world records had been broken and two others equaled. Some of the highlights included American William Carr's world record in the 400-meter race

AGRICULTURAL PARK

WILLIAM M. BOWEN

LOS ANGELES MEMORIAL COLISEUM, UNDER CONSTRUCTION

and Eddie Tolan's gold medals in both the 100- and 200-meter hurdles. Mildred "Babe" Didrickson won gold medals in the 80-meter hurdles and the javelin throw, as well as a silver medal in the high jump.

Not only did the Games attract athletes and tourists from around the globe, it also brought the world's media to Los Angeles. More than seven hundred writers arrived to cover "the world's mightiest athletic drama," as the *Los Angeles Evening Herald Express* described the Olympic Games. The Coliseum's 180-foot-long press box on the south side was one of the many innovations. A new teletype system enabled reporters to instantly transmit results to their wire services and radio stations. Insulated booths for radio broadcasting and official photographer rooms and work spaces for reporters provided a modern boost in covering one of the biggest stories of the year.

The world's attention was focused on Los Angeles and, most especially, on the grand stadium designed by John Parkinson. The Coliseum was the focal point of the Games, the site of a number of events in track and field, gymnastics, field hockey, equestrian jumping, as well as serving as the start and finish points for the marathon. In the Coliseum, spectators from around the world gathered to watch emotional ceremonies honoring newly crowned Olympic champions as they received their hard-earned medals. On these grounds, the opening ceremony featured the lighting of the iconic Olympic torch— and the excitement of the world along with it. By the end of it all, the Coliseum would bask in a final Olympic glory, hosting the closing ceremony, as the Games officially ended on Sunday, August 14.

The dream of Los Angeles becoming an international city of importance was fulfilled. A period of astonishing growth and ambition had culminated in the arrival of the world's greatest sports competition. "When we think of the Coliseum, we have to think of Los Angeles's desire to invent itself," historian Kevin Starr says. "Imagine the chutzpah of a newly emerging city, that was only one hundred thousand people twenty years earlier, wanting to compete against the great cities of the world for the Olympics, and imagine the surprise when Los Angeles won."

"THE FATHER OF OLYMPIC PARK"

The journey towards creating an Olympic venue for Los Angeles actually began as a passionate campaign to clean up an urban eyesore, a task initiated by a close friend of John Parkinson from his carefree days in Napa, California. Attorney William M. Bowen, who had once competed with Parkinson in a Napa debating society, was an emerging power in Los Angeles politics at the twilight of the nineteenth century. A deeply religious man, Bowen was determined

Parkinson's renderings for Los Angeles Memorial Coliseum

LOS ANGELES MEMORIAL COLISEUM 131

Los Angeles Memorial Coliseum, prior to Olympic Games

to uplift a once-proud area called Agricultural Park, which he argued had become a "spectacle of immorality" and corruption.

The 160-acre park, established in 1872, was originally intended for county fairs and as a venue for local farmers to showcase produce and livestock. Once owned by the state, the land had been acquired by private interests who built a racetrack, several saloons, and a hotel that Bowen claimed was a "house of ill fame." The park's location, just outside Los Angeles city limits, meant it was not subject to the city's ban on gambling. Thus, it had become a popular venue for horse and greyhound racing, as well as "coursing," a brutal sport in which rabbits were pursued and often killed by hounds. Bowen, who lived and worked nearby as a part-time teacher at the University of Southern California Methodist Church, was infuriated when he discovered some of his students were gambling in the park after Sunday-school classes, and he vowed to do something about it.

Born in Indiana during the Civil War, Bowen spent much of his childhood in Kansas. His educational opportunities were limited but he never lacked ambition and a sense of purpose. At the age of fourteen, after his father died, he moved with his mother and four sisters to a seventy-acre farm near Napa. Working long hours, he would seed and harvest the considerable property, often by himself, and still find time to pursue his studies at the Napa Collegiate Institute. John Parkinson remembered, "At the time, I lived in Napa, on a small, rocky, hillside farm, a couple of miles from town, a broad-shouldered youngster standing over six feet high lived and worked from sunrise to sunset, cultivating the soil, picking up the granite boulders and hauling them away for twenty-five cents a load and caring for a few cattle. The youngster was also road master and must see that the country roads were in good repair and generally by the use of his own big muscles. But in addition to strong arms he had brains and ambition, extending beyond the Napa Hills. His name was William M. Bowen. To the Napa boys he was Bowen. His ambition was to become a lawyer—he was as poor as Lincoln."

Bowen's first step toward a legal career began as a janitor for prominent Northern California attorney, Henry C. Gesford, who became a mentor and allowed him to study the firm's legal books outside work hours. In 1892, Bowen began studying for a law degree at Drake University in Iowa. After graduating, he and his wife Louise Martin gathered their belongings in a covered wagon and moved to Los Angeles, where he joined his older brother Calvin C. Bowen's law firm. When his brother entered the ministry in 1896, he entered into a partnership with Judge W.F. Henning.

Bowen's campaign to transform Agricultural Park began in earnest when he successfully ran for City Council in 1900. He quickly wielded his influence to investigate how the property's ownership had been

LOS ANGELES MEMORIAL COLISEUM EXTERIOR

EXPOSITION PARK, SUNKEN ROSE GARDEN

LOS ANGELES MEMORIAL COLISEUM EXTERIOR

1932 OLYMPICS, OPENING CEREMONY

LOS ANGELES MEMORIAL COLISEUM

OLYMPIC STADIUM

LOS ANGELES MEMORIAL COLISEUM EXTERIOR

134 ICONIC VISION

LOS ANGELES MEMORIAL
COLISEUM RENDERING

transferred from the State of California to private interests and soon uncovered a trail of corruption. In 1904, he filed a lawsuit in Los Angeles County Superior Court to return the park to public ownership. It was the beginning of a bitter legal battle that culminated on August 8, 1908, when the California Supreme Court ruled the land was indeed public property.

Victorious, Bowen set about beautifying the park. He created a master plan that brought together city, county, and state interests to fund its improvement. He successfully lobbied for $250,000 from the state to build an Exposition Building and also was assured a promise of funding from the county to pay for a Los Angeles Museum of History, Science and Art. Parkinson & Bergstrom was recruited in 1912 to design the sunken rose gardens. When it later came time to rename the park, many pushed for it to be called Bowen Park in recognition of his efforts. Others suggested University Park, but eventually it became known as Exposition Park.

Bowen's legal battle to transform Agricultural Park received the backing of USC President George F. Bovard, who shared his concerns about seedy activities taking place near campus. When a group of civic leaders, including the publishers of five Los Angeles newspapers, proposed building a sports stadium in the park, Bovard promised if the project was successful, the USC football team would make the venue its permanent home. Harry Chandler of the *Los Angeles Times*, Guy Barham of the *Herald*, Fred Kellogg of the *Evening Express*, Maximilian Ihmsen of the *Examiner* and H.B.R. Briggs of the *Record* put aside their differences and joined forces with the Community Development Association, an ambitious civic group originally established by Mayor Meredith P. Snyder to enhance the Spanish heritage of Los Angeles.

In the spring of 1919, the Community Development Association and its supporters began to push for the construction of a stadium in Exposition Park and a town hall, to be known as the Los Angeles Memorial Auditorium. Both structures would serve the dual purpose of providing a lasting tribute to veterans of the First World War, while also providing a venue capable of attracting conventions and tourism dollars. John Parkinson was selected as the architect for the new Coliseum, while Parkinson and John C. Austin worked together on plans for a twelve-thousand-capacity auditorium. "It was through Bowen that I became a member and served on the Park Board," Parkinson later recalled. "We had many talks about its development, and it was through Bowen that I later served as architect for the Coliseum."

A population explosion and post-war economic boom gave civic leaders the confidence to believe that if the funds could be raised to build a new stadium, the *Los Angeles Evening Herald* determined that the Olympic Games of 1924 were "a probable prize to be captured by the city." In the summer of 1920, William May Garland, president of the Community Development Association and a prominent real estate

WILLIAM M. GARLAND

OLYMPIC FEVER IN DOWNTOWN LOS ANGELES

1932 OLYMPICS OPENING CEREMONY TICKET

FANS FILL THE LOS ANGELES MEMORIAL COLISEUM

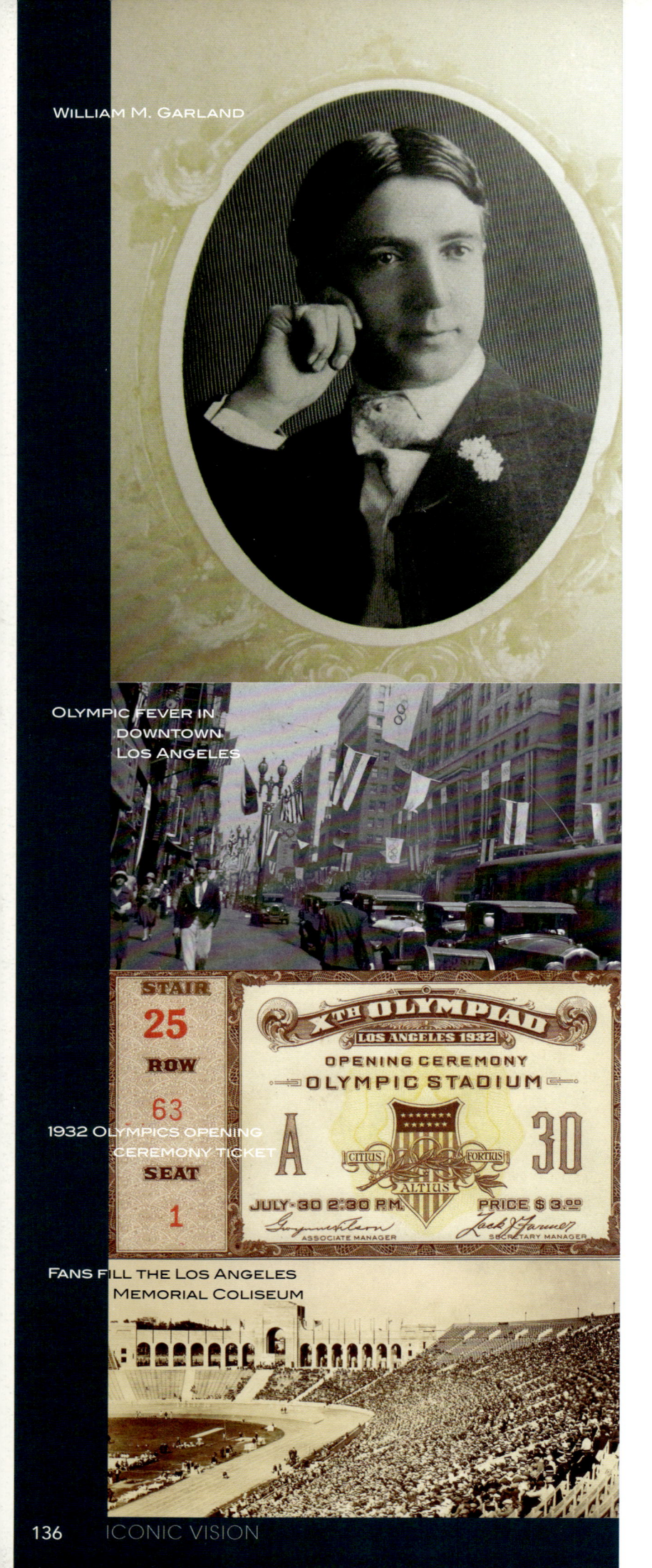

developer, traveled to Europe in hopes of convincing the Olympic Committee that Los Angeles was prepared to host the prestigious event. He carried with him Parkinson's blueprints for the Coliseum, which formed the centerpiece of his presentation. Garland later wrote to his wife, "I must say they received my invitation with a smile and informed me that they thought it would be very difficult to bring the Games to America, and certainly not to California, which was three thousand miles beyond New York!" As Garland would soon discover, a deal was already in place for the 1924 Games to be held in Paris. Furthermore, the 1928 Games had been promised to Amsterdam. Not to be deterred, he left behind a copy of Parkinson's blueprints and an invitation to stage the Games of 1932 in Los Angeles before beginning his long journey home.

While Garland was away in Europe, bond propositions were placed on the ballot to raise one million dollars for a new Coliseum and four million dollars for a Memorial Auditorium. The *Los Angeles Herald* warned voters the proposition would "test the sincerity of their professions of patriotism and sentiments of gratitude to the brave men who put down the war against humanity, and will appeal to their finer senses of pride in their city." The day before the election, The *Evening Herald* reported that Mayor Snyder issued a proclamation declaring the vote one of the most important in the city's history. He appealed to business owners who employed veterans to allow them time off to vote and to "sacrifice the profits of the day to insure the prosperity of the future."

Upon his return to Los Angeles, Garland discovered both bond propositions narrowly failed to gain the required two-thirds majority. The final tally: Auditorium, For 37,350, Against 19,088; Coliseum, For 36,039, Against 19,238. Although many voters complained the layout of the ballots had been confusing, supporters of the projects now faced the ominous task of finding private funding. Securing financial backing for a Memorial Auditorium was soon forgotten, as the Coliseum became the primary focus. Adding further impetus, Garland reported to the Community Development Association that to stand any chance of competing for the Olympics, Los Angeles needed a stadium worthy of holding such a prestigious event. The proposed stadium should, he argued, according to the *Examiner*, "be of such character as to spread the fame of the city and aid in placing Los Angeles in her proper position among the greatest cities of the world."

Although there was no guarantee the project would ever be funded, Parkinson made the Coliseum's design a top priority for his already-busy architectural practice. He viewed the ambitious

Los Angeles Memorial Coliseum at Christmastime postcard

LOS ANGELES MEMORIAL COLISEUM 137

LOS ANGELES MEMORIAL COLISEUM, DETAILS

undertaking as his civic responsibility and agreed his firm would work at cost while he donated his own services. Even after early supporters abandoned the project on the heels of the bond-proposition failure, Parkinson forged ahead. His determination inspired *Los Angeles Times* publisher Harry Chandler, who used Parkinson's plans to help convince a group of fourteen prominent bankers to underwrite construction of the stadium with an eight-hundred-thousand-dollar loan. Contractors were encouraged to keep their bids low. When it was revealed that Edwards, Wildey & Dixon Co. had submitted the lowest bid of $833,165, the firm further reduced its bid to $772,000 so that John Parkinson's $28,000 out-of-pocket expenses could be included within the original eight-hundred-thousand-dollar budget.

As a nonprofit organization, the Community Development Association announced it would take control of the stadium for the first ten years, after which the city and county would repay the construction cost in installments and eventually take over ownership. Any profit would be reinvested in the stadium and its grounds.

THE DESIGN

John Parkinson spent several months researching sports stadiums around the world before fixing his attention on an elliptical design for the Coliseum built on the sloped bank of a sand-and-gravel pit. The lowest bank of seats would be built on an excavated grade, while the next section of tiered seats would be built into a compacted berm. After a review of the Coliseum's exterior and interior design, the *Los Angeles Examiner* proclaimed the training facilities and dressing rooms would provide "all the comfort and luxury afforded in the Metropolitan Opera House." For spectators used to concrete seating at sporting events, the tiers of wooden seats were considered a luxurious addition. Early plans called for a 61-foot-high, 206-foot-wide memorial archway supported by a "wide row of classic pillars" as the entrance to the stadium and an admission gate on the Vermont Avenue side.

Groundbreaking ceremonies were held on December 21, 1920, and eight months later on August 22, 1921, Parkinson submitted the final plans to the Municipal Arts Commission, which quickly approved the design. "The plans are very finely worked out," President John W. Mitchell told the *Los Angeles Times*. "The structure will be as fine as anything in the United States—better, I think than the Yale Bowl, the Harvard Stadium, or the Columbia Stadium." Parkinson later wrote, "Many problems in the plan and construction were solved and ample provision made for expansion and

LOS ANGELES
MEMORIAL COLISEUM

1932 OLYMPICS, EVENT GUIDE

Xth OLYMPIAD
Los Angeles
1932

Complete Program of Events

Ticket Information

REVISED—FEBRUARY 1, 1932

"May the Olympic Torch Pursue its Way Through the Ages"

TICKET DEPARTMENT
Olympic Games Committee
W. M. GARLAND BUILDING, Los Angeles, California

---

contraction during changes of temperature and for earthquake stresses, which have proven entirely adequate."

By year's end, construction had begun. When the first section, including the track, was completed, Parkinson decided to test the metal of Zach Farmer, manager of the Coliseum, and L.E. Dixon, the contractor. "We stood looking down into the amphitheater with its running track at the outer edge, one-third of a mile long," Parkinson remembered. "Zach was twenty-eight, an all-round athlete; Dixon was thirty-two, a slim chap, and I was sixty-one and no longer slim, but feeling like a youngster. I challenged to race them. They instantly agreed, and off we went. Zach was over the line first running easily fifty feet ahead of Dixon, and I was fifty feet behind Dixon, going well but glad to get over the finish line…I concluded after running in the first one-third of a mile race around the new Coliseum track, that it was the right place and time for me to retire as a runner."

COLISEUM EXPANSION

Construction of the Coliseum was completed on schedule on May 1, 1923. That same year, the International Olympic Committee granted William Garland's request to bring the Olympic Games to Los Angeles in 1932. To prepare for the Games, John and Donald Parkinson were asked to work on plans to expand the stadium's capacity to 101,000 by adding an additional third tier of seating. With financing from the city and county, the expansion work got underway in February of 1930. Among the many additions to the stadium was an imposing concrete Olympic torch topped by a bronze fixture—its distinctive flame would burn brightly throughout the Games. They also created a special seating area to hold dignitaries and added a larger scoreboard.

John Parkinson served as chairman of an Olympic special architecture committee that oversaw all venues including the Pasadena Rose Bowl, Los Angeles Swimming Stadium, and Riviera Country Club. The Coliseum was temporarily renamed Olympic Stadium in anticipation of the global event. "The Los Angeles Coliseum is the largest single structure designed in our office, constructed of reinforced concrete, measuring about two-thirds of a mile on the outside, with 105,000 numbered seats with backs, and from every seat an unobstructed view of all parts of the field, with exits so numerous and conveniently placed that all of an audience of 105,000 can, without hurry or confusion, reach the exterior in less than ten minutes," Parkinson later recalled.

Los Angeles
Memorial Coliseum
seating

VICE PRESIDENT CHARLES
CURTIS OFFICIALLY OPENS
1932 OLYMPIC GAMES

1932 OLYMPIC GAMES, OPENING CEREMONY

A HISTORIC VENUE

The Coliseum officially opened in June of 1923, years before the Olympics, and went on to host an incredible array of major sports and other newsworthy events. The first football game played in the stadium took place on October 23, 1923, when USC hosted Pomona College in front of a crowd of 12,836. The dominating Trojans won the game 23-7. As George F. Bovard had promised, USC made the stadium its permanent home, and a host of noted coaches including Elmer "Gus" Henderson (1919-24) and Howard "Biff" Jones (1925-1940) led their teams out to a home field advantage. When the Dodgers baseball team moved from Brooklyn to Los Angeles in 1958, the Coliseum became its temporary home for four seasons before the team eventually moved to the city's Chavez Ravine ballpark. In 1959, the Dodgers hosted the Chicago White Sox in Game 5 of the World Series, which set a new world record for baseball attendance at 92,706.

The National Football League chose the Coliseum to be the site of the first Super Bowl in 1967, with the Green Bay Packers taking home the trophy over the Kansas City Chiefs. And the Super Bowl returned in 1973 when the Miami Dolphins triumphed over the Washington Redskins. During the NFL regular season, both the Los Angeles Raiders and the Los Angeles Rams called the stadium home, as did the Aztecs soccer team.

The Coliseum welcomed famous figures outside of sports, including Franklin D. Roosevelt, who made a presidential campaign appearance at the stadium on September 24, 1932. More than a decade later, as President Roosevelt led the U.S. during World War II, Generals George Patton, Joseph Stillwell and Jimmy Doolittle joined Admiral William F. "Bull" Halsey in the Coliseum for a massive war-bond rally on May 16, 1943.

Republican presidential candidates Wendell L. Willkie, Thomas E. Dewey and Dwight Eisenhower all held rallies at the venue, while newly elected Democratic President John F. Kennedy and Vice President Lyndon B. Johnson gave their acceptance speeches to well-wishers on July 15, 1960.

In the summer of 1963, a record crowd of 134,254 people packed the Coliseum for Billy Graham's Los Angeles Crusade for Christ. Religion proved to be a huge draw again on September 15, 1987, when more than one hundred thousand visitors turned out to see Pope John Paul II.

In more recent decades, the Coliseum welcomed music into its diverse repertoire, staging sold-out performances by famous groups, including the Rolling Stones, U2, Metallica, and Pink Floyd in front of hordes of fans.

In 1984, the Olympic Games returned to Los Angeles. The city's stadium was once again tapped to play the starring role in both the opening and closing ceremonies, this time for the world to see on television. On July 28, President Ronald Reagan officially welcomed athletes from 140 nations to the Coliseum for the Games of the XXIII Olympiad. Millions would witness Carl Lewis tie Jesse Owen's 1936 record of four gold medals; Sebastian Coe become the first man to win consecutive gold medals in the 1500-meter race; and controversy erupted when Zola Budd and Mary Decker-Slaney collided in the 3000-meter final.

In recognition of its place in the history of California and of the United States, the Coliseum was named both state and federal historical landmarks. The stadium continues to host USC Trojan football games and other events, drawing visitors from near and far to its historic grounds. The Coliseum stands as a legacy to those long ago who propelled Los Angeles to become one of the most famous and most visited cities in the world.

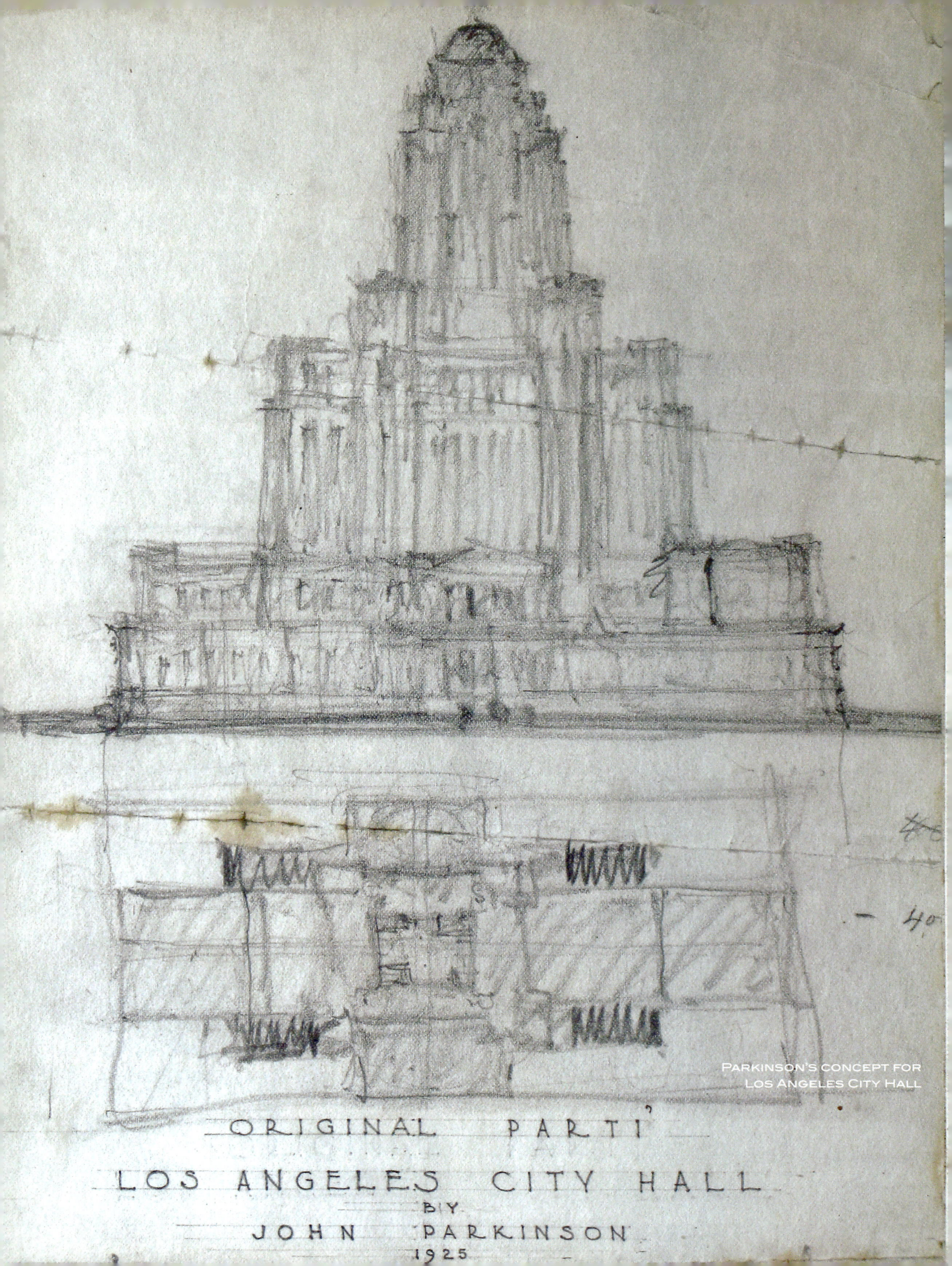

ORIGINAL PARTI
LOS ANGELES CITY HALL
BY
JOHN PARKINSON
1925

Parkinson's concept for
Los Angeles City Hall

THE BIGGEST TURNOUT THE CITY HAD EVER SEEN

THE SPIRIT OF A NEW BEGINNING WAS EVERYWHERE IN THE AIR, AND ALL OF THE MANY PEOPLE WHO PACKED THE STREETS DOWNTOWN COULD FEEL IT. The most powerful measure that Los Angeles had arrived as a city of prominence was the sheer size of the crowd that gathered to witness the formal dedication of its first monumental structure, Los Angeles City Hall. On Thursday morning, April 26, 1928, Grand Marshal Brigadier General Walter P. Story, a World War I veteran and prominent financier, waited until precisely ten o'clock to give the signal to launch the biggest civic parade ever staged in any city west of Chicago. More than a half-million cheering spectators lined the sidewalks; newspaper predictions of a turnout of seventy-five thousand vastly underestimated the public desire to witness a defining moment in the development of an ambitious young city. It was the nation's biggest public celebration since New York City feted Charles Lindbergh after his heroic solo transatlantic flight less than a year earlier, and many arrived before sunrise to ensure a good view. As a reporter for the *Evening Herald* wrote, "Shrill cries of darting children, anguished calls of distracted parents, toots of horns, shrieks of whistles and clanging of street car bells blended into a cacophony of sound."

Los Angeles had reaped the rewards of a decade of dynamic, unprecedented growth following the end of the First World War, and the city's mayor, George E. Cryer, promised citizens a new municipal building that would be "in keeping, architecturally, with the dignity and community idealism of America's most rapidly growing city." Many anticipated Los Angeles would one day become the greatest city in America. In just thirty years, the city's population had exploded tenfold from one hundred thousand to nearly 1.25 million. It was now the fifth largest city in the country, surpassing San Francisco and established East Coast cities, such as Boston, Baltimore, and Washington, D.C. Angelenos demanded a building that reflected the city's growing national and international influence.

That challenge ultimately ended up on the drafting table of John Parkinson, who envisioned the concept for the new city hall and took charge of its architectural design. The most significant landmark in Los Angeles, Parkinson's glittering City Hall was a milestone in an equally glittering career for the accomplished architect. A special exception to city law, which limited buildings to 150 feet, meant at 452 feet, the towering structure stood as an imposing statement on the city's ever-expanding skyline. Since construction began two years prior, the five-million-dollar structure had become a symbol of collective pride for the Angelenos who had keenly observed its months-long development.

The historic parade that began on the corner of Sixteenth and Hill streets featured 32,000 marchers, thirty-four bands, and scores of festooned floats. Modern-day veterans who had returned from battle in the First World War mixed with their predecessors who fought decades earlier in the Civil and Spanish American Wars. Mayor Cryer, who spearheaded the campaign to build City Hall, appealed to businesses to excuse workers taking part in the parade. Traveling north

MAYOR GEORGE E. CRYER ADDRESSES THE OPENING DAY CROWD.

LOS ANGELES CITY HALL DEDICATION-DAY PARADE

LOS ANGELES CITY HALL LIT UP BY THE LIGHTS OF MGM STUDIOS

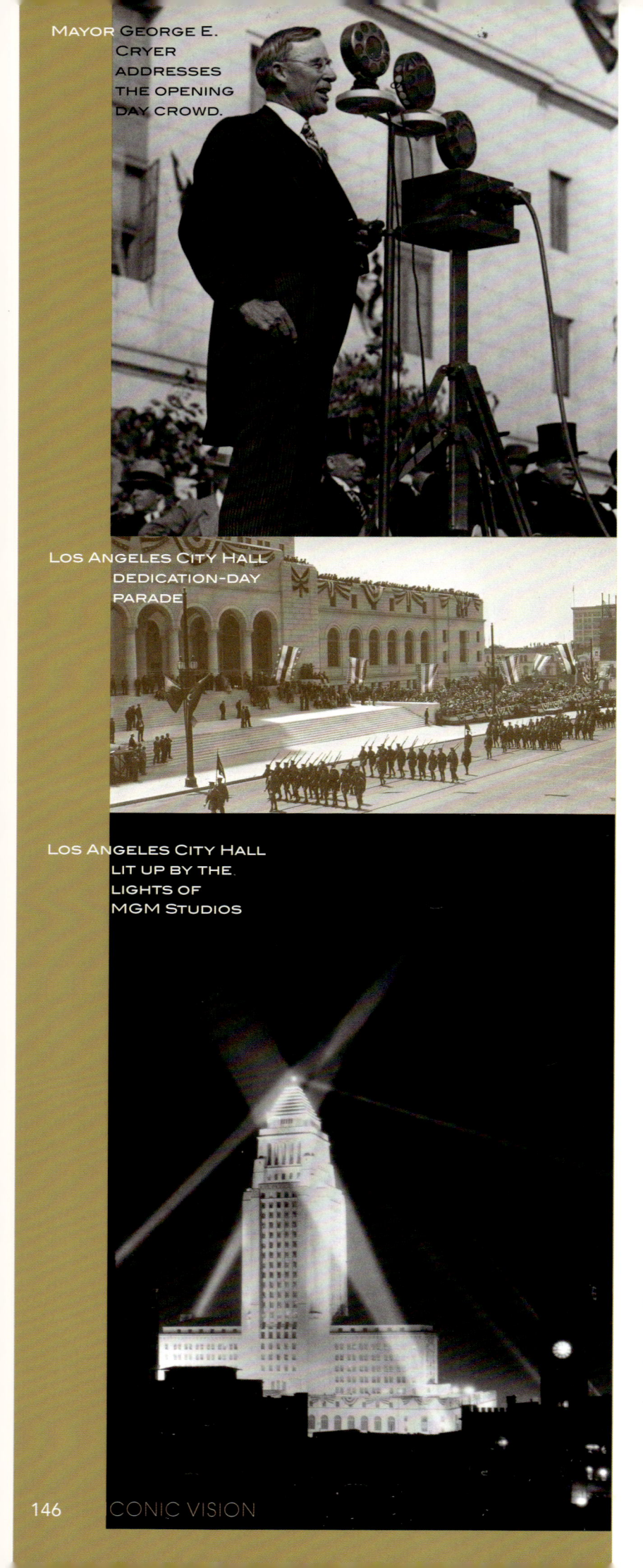

on Hill to Pico, then on to Broadway, the marchers and floats wound through streets decorated with ornate flags and banners. As the procession approached Second and Third streets, a moment of poignancy filled the frenetic air, as marchers passed by and saluted the now-retired old brownstone City Hall, patriotically dressed up for its final farewell. Its forty-year run had come to an end, and Los Angeles celebrated the start of a new era.

While the crowds generally were well-behaved, a special detail of eight hundred policemen had their hands full, according to the *Evening Herald*, stopping spectators from spilling out into the streets and keeping children from "under horse's hoofs and automobile wheels."

Many Hollywood film studios had offices downtown, so a large section of the parade was lead by celebrated director and producer, Cecil B. DeMille, who was joined by Leo, the MGM lion, and many of the leading movie stars of the day. The spectacle before parade-goers was as varied as one could imagine. Among the more popular sights in the procession was an enormous white cake in the shape of the new City Hall and a huge tiger float produced by the Chinese community. "Chinatown has done itself proud," the *Los Angeles Examiner* reported, adding that there were "More and bigger floats in this division than anywhere else in the parade." The Salvation Army was warmly applauded, as were truckloads of Red Cross nurses, California college cadets, the Boy Scouts, Ladies of the G.A.R., and the various military units who made up roughly five thousand of the marchers.

The route stretched across sixteen city blocks, a distance of three miles. The city had declared this special day a holiday for its workers. Sixteen thousand city employees marched in the parade, which ended with a procession of stagecoaches and floats, representing scenes from popular movies, a fast-growing industry in Los Angeles. Heading toward First and Spring streets, they finally arrived at the reviewing stand where microphones were installed so the entire program could be broadcast over the newly established radio station KPLA and its sister-station KYA in San Francisco.

Two hundred invited guests, including visiting mayors and city officials, gathered for lunch at the opulent Biltmore Hotel before moving on to a lavish reception at the new City Hall. Soon after, Mayor Cryer led a procession of dignitaries out of the south door of City Hall and on to the platform. And with that, the stage was set. At three o'clock, the formal dedication got underway as film producer Joseph Schenck served as master of ceremonies, and impresario Sid Grauman oversaw the entertainment. A group of singers, known as

LOS ANGELES CITY HALL DEDICATION-DAY PARADE FLOAT, COMPLETE WITH BEAUTIFUL GIRLS

the Rangers, fired pistol shots in the air and stormed down the steps before launching into song. The first speaker to step to the podium was Arthur Eldridge, president of the Board of Public Works. "If there were no other material evidence of the phenomenal progress of this community apparent to the casual observer, this monument—the new City Hall—a symbol of the communities' faith in the present and the future, this should be sufficient," he said.

Loudspeakers carried the address to surrounding areas and nearby towns. The City Parks Department broadcast the entire ceremony to crowds who gathered in all the parks on the public address system— Westlake, Exposition, Pasadena City Park, Hermosa Beach, and Venice were among the many. A Boy Scout raised the Stars and Stripes as a choir sang, "America," triggering the enormous crowd to join in the singing. "Let us this day, as we dedicate this building, make it the occasion for a re-dedication of ourselves to better and higher ideals of citizenship," Mayor Cryer began his address. Seizing the opportunity he continued, "And best of all my friends, no breath of scandal, no suggestion of graft has attended any measure of the work. This is the more remarkable because there are those in this community who do not require a basis in fact upon which to hurl a charge of wrongdoing."

As the dedication drew to a close, Irving Berlin sang some of his popular hits, and the entertainment on the steps of City Hall continued into the late afternoon. At seven o'clock in the evening, President Coolidge pressed a gold telegraph key in his White House study that illuminated the giant Colonel Charles A. Lindbergh Airway Beacon atop Los Angeles City Hall, three thousand miles west, sending its brilliant eight million-candlepower rays skyward. George L. Eastman, president of the city's chamber of commerce, read aloud a message of support from President Coolidge that began, "I wish to extend sincere congratulations to the officials and citizens of Los Angeles upon the acquisition of the beautiful new home for her city government." Pausing, Eastman continued in his own words, "The thoughts and ideals of a great city have been given material expression in steel, marble, and everlasting beauty… May this beacon guide us in the future to that great development of aviation to which we are looking."

As dusk descended on the historic celebration, MGM Studios had in place its entire supply of lighting equipment, which unleashed 12,550,000,000-beam candlepower, ensuring the new City Hall, in all its splendor, was visible for miles around. "That flood of light touched off the tremendous crowd," the Los Angeles Examiner reported. "They greeted their new City Hall as they have never before greeted anything."

The next day, Examiner reporter Harry Lang wrote, "There have been dedications in this town before; but compared with yesterday's, they loom about as impressive as would a switchman's shanty beside

CITY HALL

ICONIC VISION

Mayor George E. Cryer used a gold-plated shovel on the afternoon of March 5, 1926 to turn over the first earth on the site where the new City Hall would be built.

CITY HALL 149

LOS ANGELES CITY HALL, BROADWAY

LOS ANGELES CITY HALL, BROADWAY, LIBRARY

NEBRASKA STATE CAPITOL INSPIRES PARKINSON

JOHN C. AUSTIN WITH A MODEL OF CITY HALL

the City Hall that was dedicated." Amidst the celebration and pageantry, it would have been easy to forget the seemingly endless political strife and legal disputes that preceded the construction of City Hall—and just how difficult a journey it had all been.

THE POLITICS OF A NEW CITY HALL

Los Angeles City Hall owes its location on the corner of Spring and Temple streets to a 1907 report produced by Charles Mulford Robinson. A city planner from Rochester, New York, Robinson was a leading advocate of the City Beautiful movement, a philosophy that grew out of the idea that the beautification of cities would improve their moral and civic virtues. Between 1860 and 1910, the number of cities in America with more than one hundred thousand residents grew from eight to fifty, sparking fears that inadequate planning could leave vast urban areas shapeless, ugly, and uninspiring. Robinson was recruited by the Los Angeles Municipal Arts Commission, of which John Parkinson was a founding member, to produce a master plan for the city. "In this garden region and home of the well-to-do and cultured, and the newest section to have urban development—it is least pardonable that there should be ugliness where beauty should be," Robinson ranted to the *Los Angeles Times*.

In his report, Robinson recommended a large municipal administrative center where public buildings would be grouped, as the best way to create a unifying focal point for the city. The following year, the city council approved a plan to purchase a lot on Spring Street specifically for this purpose. Although Robinson's plan was never fully implemented, it remained an influential idea in the minds of politicians.

Between 1900 and 1920, the population of Los Angeles expanded five hundred percent to nearly six hundred thousand residents. As the population grew, so did frustration over the inadequate facilities offered by City Hall on Broadway, built in 1888, when Angelenos numbered less than fifty thousand. A general lack of confidence in its design led to fears vital city records could be lost if the building caught fire or collapsed. In 1903, the city hired John Parkinson and John C. Austin to determine if the tower was in danger of falling as a result of the building being overloaded. In their review, the architects concluded it could be made safe by adding columns for support for the Library Room. According to Parkinson, "If this room was crowded with people, their weight, in addition to the books, would be fifty per cent more than this kind of construction is expected to uphold."

THE NEW LOS ANGELES
CITY HALL

NEW CITY HALL LOS
#7 4/1/27 S.W. COR
Foster and Kleiser
More Room – More Comfort
More Value
DODGE BROTHERS
MOTOR CARS

A California granite façade was used on the first three floors of the new City Hall. The façades above the third floor are matte-glazed terra cotta.

THE NEW CITY HALL CONSTRUCTION TOWERS OVER THE CITY

LOS ANGELES CITY HALL COLUMNED PORTICO

Nearly two decades passed, but nothing was done. Numerous attempts to reinvigorate Robinson's original plan for a civic center ran out of steam in a climate of political acrimony and economic uncertainty caused by the onset of the First World War. As Los Angeles entered the 1920s, a movement to build a new city hall gained traction and found its biggest supporter yet in the city's newly elected mayor, George E. Cryer.

In 1921, Cryer came to power, promising to clean up politics in Los Angeles. A quiet-yet-effective politician, his campaign slogan was, "A Big Man for a Big City," and he needed to live up to this boast to overcome the constant bickering that had become business as usual between his predecessor, Meredith Snyder, and the city council. Born in 1875 on a farm in Douglas County, Nebraska, Cryer's parents moved to Los Angeles when he was ten. A veteran of the Spanish American War and a seasoned lawyer, he was forty-six-years-old when elected. Once in power, he quickly took up the fight to build a new administration center, including a new city hall, and within two years, managed to persuade the electorate to approve five million dollars in bonds for the project and $2,500,000 for the purchase of land.

HOW THE ARCHITECTS WERE CHOSEN

The search to find an architect for City Hall began in earnest in the fall of 1923 when the Board of Public Works, responsible for the construction and maintenance of public buildings, held a meeting with a panel of architects, including John Parkinson and John C. Austin. A statewide competition would be open to all California architects, and the rules would be determined by a special committee. Two architects from the Los Angeles-based Allied Architects Association plus Parkinson and Austin made up the committee, which then selected a fifth member, W.B. Faville, president of the American Institute of Architects.

The competition was announced a week before a long-planned city council conference to discuss the layout and construction of civic center buildings. The *Examiner* reported that city council members balked at the idea, accusing the board of being "discourteous" for acting entirely on its own. And thus began a rift that would threaten to divide those who ran the city. In the year that followed, the council and board became immersed in a relentless battle of opposing wills. Both sides argued endlessly over who had the right to select an architect for the project and the exact location of the building.

As the politicians squabbled, Parkinson returned home to

England where he visited relatives in Bolton. He took time to reconnect with Joe Glazebrook with whom his North American adventure had begun almost forty years before, and he found him working as a carpenter at a cotton mill. "He seemed very old at sixty-three," Parkinson later reflected. "He died about two years later. I found a number of those I had known as a youngster, all well along in years. I wondered, am I an old man like these chaps?"

When Parkinson returned to Los Angeles, he found little had changed. Councilman Walter Mallard, who had taken a keen interest in the City Hall argument, expressed fears the process of selecting an architect was already corrupted. "Almost every American city has had trouble in building a city hall," he complained in the *Los Angeles Times*. "I hoped for quick action here and a wide-open competition for the plans, and everyone satisfied. We hear all kinds of rumors. One is that an illegal, crooked deal has been made whereby five or six architects are to be told to prepare plans, two or three of them will get the work, and then those that get the contract will split the three-hundred-thousand-dollar commission with those who did not work, but keep quiet." Fearing the councilman was pointing the finger at them, the Allied Architects membership quickly denied any such deal existed.

The council and the board searched for ways to break the deadlock. The council sought advice and sent a telegram to the offices of the *Chicago Tribune*, where a designer for its new building had recently been selected. Members of the board suggested Chief Building Inspector J.J. Backus take a leave of absence and design the new city hall himself. Others called for the Allied Architects Association to be awarded the contract, while some pushed for the formidable trio of John Parkinson, John C. Austin, and Albert C. Martin who, combined, had designed more the eighty million dollars of Los Angeles structures and were ready to cooperate on a joint bid. Both the Allied Architects Association and the team of Parkinson, Austin, and Martin submitted offers to the board shortly before Christmas of 1924.

Less than two months later, in February and without warning, the city council made the surprise announcement they were officially backing the firm of Curtlett & Beelman to design the new civic headquarters, even though the firm hadn't submitted a bid or even publicly expressed any interest in the project. The decision came as a shock to everyone, including Curtlett & Beelman, whose most notable work was the Elks Lodge on Park View Street. "We knew nothing of the City Hall plan until shortly before noon, when we were notified that our firm had been selected as architects," Alexander E. Curtlett told the *Los Angeles Times*. "As a result we have no definite ideas on the structure and will not have until the proposition is given a thorough study." Council President Boyle Workman explained, "The Councilmen expressed the desire to get started on planning the new City Hall, and the selection of Curtlett & Beelman expressed the Council's determination to secure architects of standing who were not identified with either the Allied Architects Association or the so-called

LOS ANGELES CITY HALL,
RENDERING

independents, both of which groups had been active in the controversy over the planning of the City Hall."

The council's decision infuriated members of the board, who fired off an angry letter to the council insisting the more experienced team of Parkinson, Austin, and Martin get the job. Upon receiving the correspondence, Workman called members of the council and the board into a secret meeting in his office. Outside, lobbyists waited anxiously for any developments, but after an hour, both sides emerged without a breakthrough. City Attorney Jess E. Stephens, who attended the meeting, was assigned the difficult task of determining which of the two entrenched sides had the legal authority to make the decision.

A new city charter, scheduled to take effect in July, would give more power to the mayor. The charter also made it clear that when it came to constructing public buildings, the Board of Public Works should supervise the construction and ultimately was responsible for the design. The longer the deadlock continued, it became evident that if all else failed, the board could simply wait it out. The council determined that if it didn't act fast, it would lose the battle, and on the advice of the city attorney, council members made the decision to enter into a contract with Curtlett & Beelman as soon as legally possible. The city would have to pay a fee of three hundred thousand dollars, or six percent of the five-million-dollar construction cost.

The council's unilateral decision provoked a hostile response from the board, which publicly refused to authorize any payment. Instead, board members set their own April 8 deadline for the submission of architectural bids and received four quotes. Later that day, rumors began swirling the new City Hall project would go to Parkinson, Austin, and Martin, and the rumors proved well-founded. The next day, the board voted unanimously to accept the architects' proposal. Under the terms of the deal, the trio was required to submit preliminary sketches and drawings within three months, and once these were accepted, they had five months to complete the final plans. The matter was referred to the city attorney for approval, though many doubted he would sign off on the deal.

The following month, Curtlett & Beelman submitted an invoice for ten thousand dollars as the first installment of their fee, and the council referred the paperwork to their finance department. It was the latest installment in what the *Los Angeles Times* referred to as a "comedy drama" of "Who is to build City Hall and if so, when?" City Auditor John S. Myers declined to pay Curtlett & Beelman a nickel until the city attorney ruled on whether their contract was legal.

LOS ANGELES CITY HALL COUNCIL CHAMBER

THE THIRD FLOOR SESSION ROOM OF THE BOARD OF PUBLIC WORKS

A.C. MARTIN, ARCHITECT

C.J. KUBACH, CONTRACTOR

JOHN C. AUSTIN, ARCHITECT

The city's much publicized rollercoaster drama made it all the way to California Superior Court, that ultimately ruled the contract with Curtlett & Beelman was invalid. Immediately, the firm threatened legal action seeking damages of $100,000 to $150,000. The city attorney and council president were appointed to a special committee to confer with the architects and their attorney, in an attempt to dissuade them from pursuing their grievances in court. Several compromises were considered, including asking Curtlett & Beelman to meet with Parkinson, Austin, and Martin to see if they could thrash out an agreement amongst themselves. Speaking out publicly on the heated debate, Mayor Cryer made it clear he favored the new contract awarded to Parkinson, Austin, and Martin.

In order to protect the city against any legal action by Curtlett & Beelman, the mayor and Board of Public Works insisted a fifty-thousand-dollar bond should be put up by Parkinson, Austin, and Martin as insurance. The city attorney agreed to approve the bond and moved to draft the board's contract with the architects. That same day, the New York firm of Schultze and Weaver, which had designed Los Angeles's Biltmore Theater, Biltmore Hotel, the Subway Terminal Building, and the Jonathan Club, sent a telegram to Mayor Cryer offering to work on plans for City Hall, but to no avail. On August 17, 1925, John Parkinson (concept/architectural design), John C. Austin (working drawings) and Albert C. Martin (structural design) were commissioned to build a new Los Angeles City Hall. Under the terms of the proposed deal, the architects would receive six percent of the five-million-dollar cost of the building, and they would complete the massive project under the supervision of the Board of Public Works.

THE "MODERN AMERICAN" DESIGN

The spirit of visionary architecture to inspire the masses abounded in the summer of 1925. The city council considered several elaborate plans for a civic center complex submitted by Lloyd Wright, son of Frank Lloyd Wright, as well as the Allied Architects Association, and the firm of Cook & Hall.

Parkinson, Austin, and Martin submitted their preliminary designs for City Hall on September 25 and won high praise from the Board of Public Works, which remarked on the "excellent" appearance of the building. Mayor Cryer was equally pleased and particularly delighted at how speedily the designs had been delivered. With early rave reviews starting to trickle in, the architects released a statement explaining their vision. "Rather than follow closely any of the so-called 'styles of architecture' of the past, the architects for the new City Hall have adapted the details and forms, chiefly of Italian Renaissance, to a modern steel-frame building. As with all good architecture, the exterior is a simple expression of the building's plan. This is the only way to achieve real beauty in architecture as well as economy and efficiency," they explained, as reported in the *Los Angeles Times*. The plans revealed the exterior of the building to be divided into three distinct sections, beginning with a light-colored California granite-clad base, ascending to the parapet above the fourth story.

A terra cotta-clad tower stretched up to a ceremonial reception room and observation deck, before the building's top section culminated in an exotic pyramidal roof at its apex, a highly visible tribute to the Mausoleum of Halicarnassus, aimed at inspiring a public mesmerized by ancient Egyptian culture at the time.

Below, the building featured Grecian detail for the main entrance and Romanesque influence in the arcades of the forecourt rotunda and Council Chamber. Still, the Parkinson team was adamant the main body of the building be regarded as "Modern American." The set-back style drew obvious comparisons to Bertram Grosvenor Goodhue's design for the Nebraska State Capitol, which had been under construction since 1922. "The monumental character of the new Los Angeles City Hall will be obtained almost entirely by means of silhouette, structural form and scale," the architects' statement continued. "Decoration will be confined to the lower stories on the exterior, where it may be easily seen and appreciated by the public."

It was expected the building's decoration would pay homage to the city's history while interior decoration would be confined to the main floor and the great central rotunda, the entrance, and the public audience rooms.

Finally, after months of a relentless political tug-of-war, the project was now underway, but not everyone was ready to bury the hatchet. In October, the city council refused to pay $54,000 in fees due to the architects for the preliminary drawings. In a bid to keep the peace, Mayor Cryer addressed the council to make it clear that neither he nor the Board of Public Works felt it necessary to rush payment to the architects. "This is a harmony administration characterized by teamwork," he explained. Harmony, however, was in short supply, as the councilmen further debated the matter. "Why the stampede to pay

JOHN AND DONALD PARKINSON STAND BEHIND GOVERNOR CLEMENT C. YOUNG AND MAYOR GEORGE E. CRYER AT A CEREMONY TO LAY THE CORNERSTONE FOR THE NEW CITY HALL

CITY HALL FROM BUNKER HILL

JOHN PARKINSON

this money?" questioned Councilman Ralph L. Criswell. "I want to be shown that this 430-foot building can be built by the Board of Public Works for the $4,500,000 set as the limit of the Board of Public Works leaving five hundred thousand dollars of the five-million-dollar bond issues for contingencies." "That's it—delays, delays," Councilman R. S. Sparks responded. "That's why the former city council could not get the new City Hall started." "Aw, sit down!" Councilman Criswell countered; the back-and-forth was quoted in the *Los Angeles Times*. The issue was finally put to a vote. The city council voted 8-3 in favor of the payment.

The construction of a twenty-eight-story building would require an exception to the city's 150-foot height restriction. The exception would have to be allowed by voters, and in case they said no, the architects simultaneously worked on plans for a much smaller structure that conformed to city law. A.C. Martin made the case in local newspapers that the nearby Hall of Justice, which stood at a higher elevation, would dwarf a smaller city hall, which might also be eclipsed by future government buildings. A smaller structure would also be significantly more expensive as it would require more ornamental stone or terra cotta, compared to a taller building that would require costly material only around the sides of the first three floors.

CONSTRUCTION BEGINS

Despite the threat of rain, an enthusiastic crowd of more than five thousand turned out for the official groundbreaking ceremony for the new Los Angeles City Hall on March 4, 1926. At 3:25 in the afternoon, a brass band played festive tunes, as Mayor Cryer thrust a ceremonial gold-plated shovel into the dirt where the ornate five-story Bullard Block had once stood. He spoke to the crowd earlier, "It is our greatest hope that we can give the city of Los Angeles an efficient City Hall that will stand for years as a monument to the citizens of this community." Representing the architects, John C. Austin revealed the project's plans were now eighty percent complete, and contracts for the steel and excavation work had been awarded. The following month, voters overwhelmingly approved Proposition 7, which called for a charter amendment to allow the new City Hall to exceed the law's 150-foot cap. *The Los Angeles Times* had reviewed Prop 7, and predicted the new building would be "sufficient to meet the needs of the public and city departments for nearly a quarter of a century."

Work on the foundations began in early May, and when the concrete was poured over two days in June, a crew of more than six hundred workers was required. The building's plans were given the blessing of the Municipal Arts Commission, which praised the architects for "designing a structure for beauty as well as usefulness at a minimum cost."

In July, workers began construction of the structure's massive steel frame, and over the next seven months, fifty tons of steel would be set in place—almost daily. In the end, more than seven thousand tons of steel worth $750,000 was supplied by the firm, McClintock Marshall.

On the afternoon of June 23, 1927, a milestone moment arrived for Los Angeles City Hall. California Governor Clement C. Young joined Mayor Cryer and other city officials for a ceremony to lay the cornerstone for the much-anticipated structure. Several thousand spectators gathered along the west front and hundreds more were on hand, peering from windows of the neighboring Hall of Records and lawn of the courthouse.

Sand from every county in California and water from all the missions were used to make a symbolic cement, supplied by every cement plant in the state. Engraved silver trowels were presented to Mayor Cryer and Governor Young who spread the special mortar just before the cornerstone was lowered into place. Inside was placed a time capsule containing several items, including a Los Angeles telephone directory, a 1927-28 City Budget and various newspapers. Mayor Cryer told the crowd, "May this great white shaft towering up toward the heavens be a beacon which will inspire one people to better things in municipal affairs." Governor Young added, "I have known Los Angeles for the last thirty years, and in that time your city's growth has been so stupendous as to stagger the imagination."

Much like Bertram Grosvenor Goodhue had done with the Los Angeles Public Library, the city hall architects would employ a team of artists and craftsmen to provide an ideological program of decoration. Parkinson and his partners hired sculptors Casper Gruenfield, Carlo Gerrone, and Henry Lion, along with mural artists Herman Sachs and Anthony Heinsbergen, to bring their vision to life. Austin Whittlesey was in charge of the overall interior design, including the Byzantine rotunda. In all, forty-six different types of marble from Europe and America were used in the decoration of the hallways and rooms.

City Hall was completed ahead of schedule and under budget. The Board of Public Works issued a resolution recognizing the work of Parkinson, Austin, and Martin. "The architects are commended by the board for the eminently satisfactory and beautiful design of the monumental building and for the efficiency displayed by them in supervising the creation of the building so that it was completed expeditiously and economically." For their services, the architects were paid six percent of the final cost of the project—a fee of $315,027.

On April 13, Mayor Cryer locked the door of his office in the old

COLONEL CHARLES A. LINDBERGH AIRWAY BEACON ATOP CITY HALL

JOHN PARKINSON

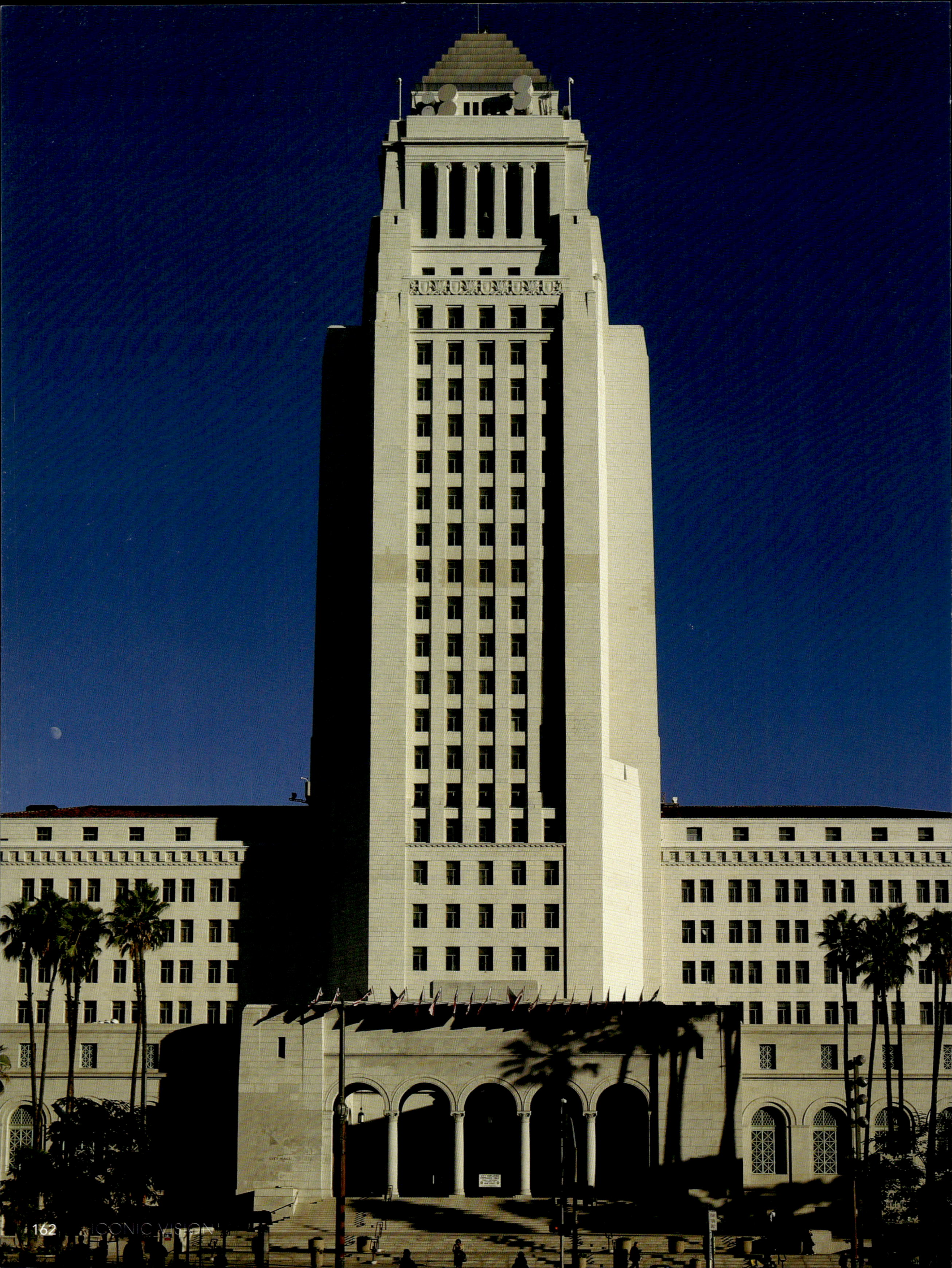

ENTRANCE TO FORECOURT

brownstone City Hall on Broadway for the last time. Rather than feeling sentimental about saying goodbye, the mayor and the majority of the city council had broad smiles on their faces, and some even cheered. "I don't care if I never come back," the mayor was heard to say (and the *Examiner* took the opportunity to capture his double negative in print), as he turned the key in the lock of his old office. Councilmen gathered up their belongings and any souvenirs they could find. After a final meeting, some of the more senior council members lingered for a last look at the place where so many political battles had played out. They were soon hurried out by a swarm of workmen tasked with clearing the building. This new Los Angeles City Hall officially became the permanent home of city government on Monday April 16, 1928. City council held its first meeting the next morning. John Parkinson, John C. Austin, and Albert C. Martin were congratulated on all sides for their work.

CITY HALL

Bullock's Wilshire

A VISIT TO THE MOST GLAMOROUS CITY IN THE WORLD, PARIS, IN 1925 WOULD COMPLETELY AFFECT THE DESIGN OF ONE OF THE MOST GLAMOROUS DESTINATIONS IN LOS ANGELES—BULLOCK'S WILSHIRE. The area's most visionary and jaw-dropping landmark ushered in a new era of the urban store, transforming the way the city shopped by embracing a thoroughly modern type of customer, the motorist. It also set a precedent for Art Deco architecture in Los Angeles and remains perhaps among the best examples of its execution in America.

When retail magnate John G. Bullock hired John and Donald Parkinson to design a new store for an undeveloped plot of land on Wilshire Boulevard, he demanded, "art and utility for the common ends of service and expression." What John and Donald Parkinson delivered surpassed all expectations and left architecture critics awestruck. Never before in Los Angeles had modern art been so masterfully woven into the design of a commercial establishment. The beige-and-green structure, with its ten-story tower, spoke to the highest ideals of what Los Angeles architecture could be. It instantly captured the city's imagination and became an essential shopping destination for Hollywood's elite.

Historian Kevin Starr explains, "Here is a building that is at once a piece of engineering and practical department store construction, but also it is a total sculpture. It is an Art Deco sculpture announcing—almost like a piece of music, almost like a leitmotif—the Great Gatsby decade, the great development of Los Angeles in a westward direction."

Excitement over the city's newest jewel abounded on September 26, 1929. At exactly nine o'clock in the morning, Bullock's Wilshire opened its doors for business for the first time, and an endless stream of shoppers flooded in to see the store for themselves. Hours before it even opened, automobiles began lining several blocks of Wilshire Boulevard as excited visitors converged in an atmosphere more akin to a lively social function than to a store opening. The *Los Angeles Times* estimated as many as three hundred thousand people came to explore what one critic later described as a "contemporary cathedral of commerce."

Whether entering on Wilshire Boulevard or through the motor court, shoppers arrived in the high domed marble foyer that gave them an immediate impression of the building's daring artistic elegance. Everywhere they looked, their eyes were drawn to unique artistic displays intended to entice shoppers. The walls of the grand perfume hall were lined with light panels accented with vertical metal strips, further adding to the moderne mood.

"Our venture into the field of applied art had its obstacles," John G. Bullock explained. "'You can't sell goods in a store that looks like an art museum,' some of our friends told us. People will be afraid of the place for fear the prices will be too high.

"To counteract any such feeling—if any existed—we have accompanied our expressions of modern art with a definite campaign of friendliness. We had to show our customers that in expanding into a new building, the old Bullock's had lost none of its intimate touch with patrons."

As they moved inside, shoppers found six eye-catching elevator doors decorated with ornate patterns in brass, copper, and gunmetal, ready to transport them to each of the five floors. Every

BULLOCK'S DEPARTMENT STORE

DESIGN FOR A BRIDGE OVER ST. VINCENT'S COURT TO JOIN TWO DOWNTOWN L.A. BULLOCK'S STORES

"AUGUST CLEARANCE" ATTRACTS A THRONG DOWNTOWN, 1919

BULLOCK'S WINDOW FASHION

department had its own unique architectural identity and yet, thanks to clever color schemes, felt connected to the whole. To the east was the accessory room, decorated in a powerful azure blue with dramatic Spanish red highlights, where stunning tubular chandeliers hung from the ceiling. Nearby, an octagonal room was devoted to shoes, its floors covered with patterned accent rugs designed by French Cubist artist, Sonya Delauney.

"As one goes from floor to floor, from room to room, there is an ever changing, never repeating, succession of novel effects, a shifting, shimmering blend of suave color and harmonies, of fabrics and glass and metal and wood combined on a painter's palette," Harris Allen wrote in *California Arts and Architecture* magazine.

To the west was the modern sportswear department dominated by a Gjura Stojana mural, "Spirit of Sports." Next door was the Saddle Shop where Jock Peters envisioned panels to give the appearance of stable stalls. Mayer Kreif's joyful plaster reliefs added personality to the walls. A doggery offered canine accessories, while the design for the menswear department paid clever tribute to Frank Lloyd Wright's concrete block architecture. "The old box architecture is over," *California Arts and Architecture* critic Pauline G. Schindler raved after exploring Bullock's Wilshire. "Each unit here is designed not alone as an individual item, but in relation to the whole. There is a fine organic integration, a harmony of thousands of individual parts." The store was, she insisted, "a significant contribution to the culture of our generation" that would "affect a revolutionary development in taste in southern California which will eventually penetrate to the more conservative north, and will strongly modify the development of architecture."

On the second floor, fashion designers offered the latest dresses and hats in extravagant salons. The Directoire Room featured exquisite formal evening wear as did the adjoining regal Louis XVI Room. In the Fur Atelier, walls of cork contrasted with the dramatic black-and-gray tiled floor, while in the lingerie boutique indirect light reflected from golden mirrors. The third floor was dedicated to clothes for college and high school girls, and the fourth floor, designed by David Collins, was filled with children's clothes, a toy room, and areas where children could play while their parents shopped. On the fifth floor, guests could meet in the splendor of the tearoom and tea patios, or inside the Desert Lounge and Cactus Room, where a Herman Sachs painted-glass ceiling represented a desert view.

"It's almost sacrilege to call it a 'store,'" Alma Whitaker

John G. Bullock (center) and
Arthur Letts (right) oversee work
on a 1917 Parkinson-designed
addition to original Bullock's store.

Bullock's Wilshire, rendering

gushed in the *Los Angeles Times*. Rather, she suggested it was a "temple to the pioneering faith of the West that epitomizes our almost spiritual faith in our destiny." William I. Garren of *Architect and Engineer* later wrote, "The success of this particular store from a merchandising standpoint aside from architecture, is clearly shown in the crowds surging around the building at night and through the day and that all California is talking about it."

Fears that early visitors would be more interested in looking than spending proved unfounded as sales staff reported "tremendous" opening-day business.

A DESIGN INSPIRED IN PARIS

John and Donald Parkinson's original plans for Bullock's Wilshire were scrapped after Donald Parkinson attended the Exposition of Industrial and Decorative Arts in Paris in 1925. Seeking inspiration, he traveled to the French capital with Percy Winnett, vice president and general manager of the Bullock's retail empire. Winnett was a regular visitor to the Paris couture houses of Schiaparelli and Chanel, and his taste for high fashion complemented Parkinson's artistic flair. What they soon discovered was too irresistible to ignore.

The Exposition had originally been intended for 1915, but was delayed due to the First World War. When the event finally took place, it drew an estimated sixteen million visitors. A host of nations provided various exhibits, but it was obvious to many that one style in particular dominated those produced by the French. Characterized by ziggurats, sunbursts, lightning flashes, and spirals, and influenced by ancient Egyptian and Mayan culture and African and Japanese art, it was sumptuous, elegant, and embraced the machine age. Influential designers such as Brandt, Lalique, Iribe, and Ruhlmann had incorporated it into their work, and it appeared in a variety of everyday household objects, including crockery, cabinets, curtains and furniture.

Parkinson and Winnett witnessed firsthand the coming of age of what would become known as Art Deco, an upbeat style created in the excitement of the Jazz Age of the 1920s and flourished through the Great Depression, a decade later. Unlike other art movements that promoted social philosophies, Art Deco was purely decorative and had only infrequently been applied to architecture prior to the Exposition. However, knowing the entire exposition site would be razed at its conclusion, French architects freely experimented with radical architectural forms and new building materials.

BULLOCK'S WILSHIRE EXTERIOR

THE 1925 PARIS EXPOSITION INSPIRED DONALD PARKINSON.

AN EARLY DESIGN FOR BULLOCK'S WILSHIRE INCLUDED AN ENTRANCE UNDERNEATH A CANOPY.

THE COMPLETED PORTE CORCHERE

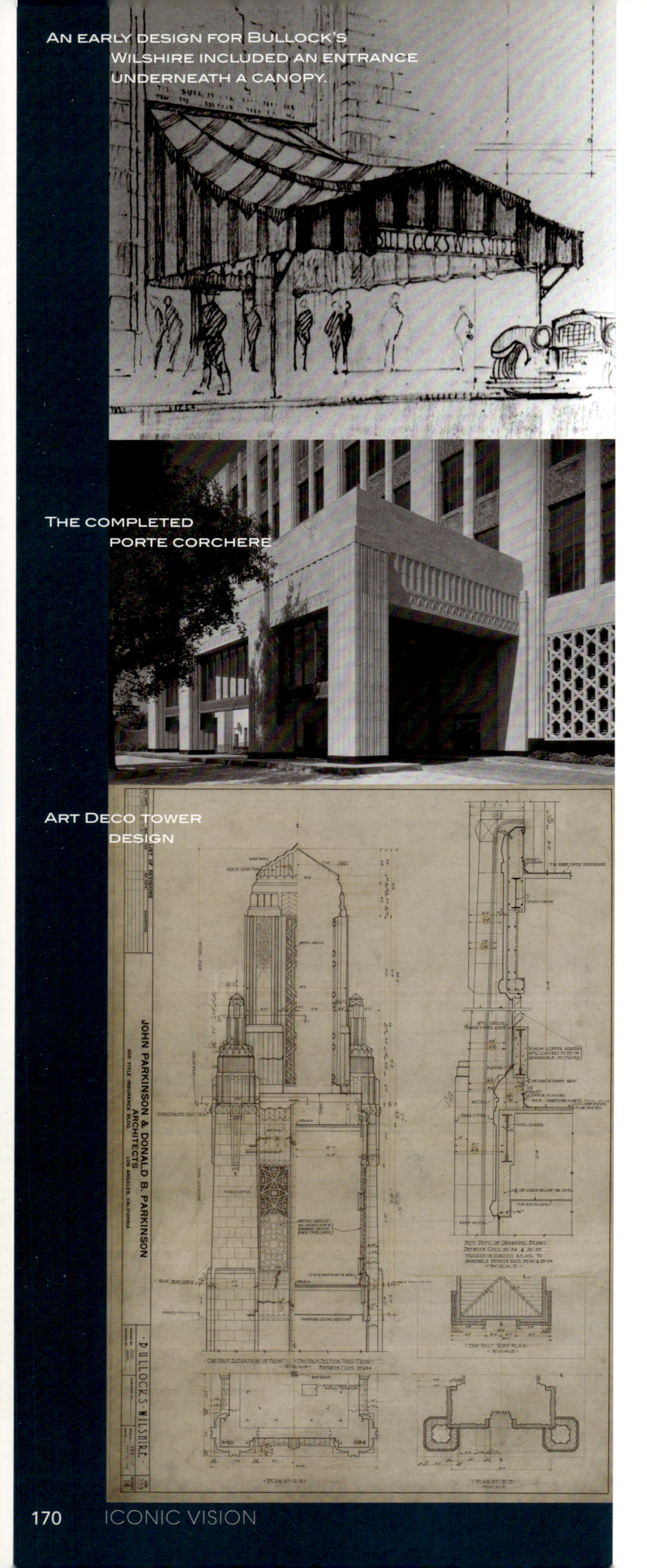

ART DECO TOWER DESIGN

Returning to the United States, Parkinson and Winnett were determined to convince their senior partners to allow them to incorporate the new style into the design for a long-planned Wilshire Boulevard store. As architectural historian Thomas S. Hines explains, "Many buildings later called Art Deco after the fair claimed ancestry to the fair, but Bullock's Wilshire grew out of it."

The completed building stretched across 294.5 feet of Wilshire Boulevard and 153.2 feet along Westmoreland and Wilshire Place providing 198,889 square feet of floor space. Its design, an adaptation of the popular American set-back style, featured steel-frame construction and a beige terra cotta-clad exterior brought to life by green, oxidized-copper panels in modern zigzag designs.

"In designing the Bullock's Wilshire building, it was our desire to use metal in plastic form for the ornamental portions, and for the tower, in combination with masonry, in order to accent the vertical lines of the building, and to add interest to the façade, which might otherwise become quite monotonous on account of its extent," John and Donald Parkinson explained in a statement.

"On account of the beautiful color, the natural variation in tone, together with its permanence and workability, we adopted copper without hesitation. The verde antique finish was developed by the use of acids, so that when the building was finished, the final color effect was established. The color tones, we believe will improve with natural weathering."

The structure began at opposite sides at two-story height, then graduated into a three- and then four-story structure in the middle. In order to maximize the building's advertising potential, the architects designed a 241-foot tower that soared above the five-story main block. The city's building ordinance set a strict 150-foot limit, however the law allowed for six feet of roof construction, thirty-five feet of penthouse construction, and fifty feet of sign construction. So Parkinson & Parkinson and builder P.J. Walker Company took full advantage. Atop the tower, a mercury beacon was installed to further command attention, and after dark, eighty-eight spotlights brought the building to shimmering life.

Along with its eye-catching beauty, Bullock's Wilshire helped usher in a new era through its embrace of the automobile. Bullock's main entrance was at the rear of the store—a novel concept at the time—and clients drove through magnificent decorative bronze gates leading to the impressive glass-walled porte cochere. Upon arrival, visitors were greeted by a small army

BULLOCK'S WILSHIRE, UNDER
CONSTRUCTION

No. 14 Taken 5-15-29

BULLOCK'S WILSHIRE BUILDING
JOB No. 384

JOHN PARKINSON &
DONALD B. PARKINSON
ARCHITECTS

P. J. WALKER CO.
BUILDERS

The Perfume Hall showcased international scents.

172 ICONIC VISION

of courteous uniformed employees standing underneath Herman Sachs' fresco-secco mural, *Speed of Transportation,* that gracefully embraced the glamour of travel featuring a montage of zeppelins, airplanes, and trains. Automobiles were parked in an adjacent parking lot behind the store. The store's enormous show windows facing Wilshire Boulevard featured carefully constructed displays deliberately positioned to attract the attention of passing motorists.

German-born designer Jock D. Peters, working with the firm of Feil & Paradise, created much of the interior design, while Eleanor LeMaire, who designed the displays in the Bullock's downtown store, lent her styling genius in the selection of carpets and draperies throughout the building and the choice of other materials used. Unlike the downtown store, the new property on Wilshire would showcase only "the most exclusive attire, luxurious gifts, toilet articles, and other things dear to the feminine heart," according to the *Los Angeles Evening Herald.*

BULLOCK'S WILSHIRE BOULEVARD GAMBLE

The decision to build a department store on Wilshire Boulevard was a gamble. In 1928 when construction began, development on Los Angeles's most celebrated thoroughfare was sporadic, and critics questioned how investing in real estate more than two miles away from the established trading areas downtown could pay off. John G. Bullock, however, was convinced the right combination of art and quality merchandise would attract customers from as far away as Pasadena and Santa Monica, as well as the wealthy residents of nearby Hancock Park and Adams Boulevard. "It is the first time a prime factor in the merchandising life of a great city has set up a rival business to itself in another part of town, inviting thereby, if successful, the certain establishing of an additional shopping center," the *Los Angeles Times* reported. The same paper would later describe Bullock's Wilshire as the "first major specialty store ever built in the suburbs of a city."

Born in the Canadian town of Paris, Ontario in 1871, John G. Bullock learned early that success came through hard work and making the most of opportunities. His father was a railroad worker and died when Bullock was two. At age eleven, he began working in a local store to help support his family. In January 1896, Bullock moved to Los Angeles where he was given a job as a salesman by Englishman Arthur Letts, founder of Los Angeles-based The Broadway department store. It would prove to be the beginning of a powerful partnership. When Letts expanded his business with a second department store in 1907, he chose Bullock to run it, and even named it after his protégé in order to keep it separate from his existing enterprise. John Parkinson was given the task of designing the store, which became one of the most profitable in Los Angeles. After two decades of steady success, Bullock was ready for a new challenge.

WILSHIRE BOULEVARD'S ART DECO MASTERPIECE ATTRACTED SHOPPERS WEST OF DOWNTOWN.

Men's Wear paid tribute to the concrete block houses designed by Frank Lloyd Wright.

"We are enjoying a splendid business. Our expansion to Wilshire Boulevard is evidence of our appreciation of the friendship and support that has been given us so generously and our determination to go forward and to do all that we can to make Bullock's of utmost service to its public," Bullock told the *Los Angeles Times* in April 1928, adding, "The growth of our city has been as remarkable as it has been substantial and it has been the endeavor of Bullock's to keep pace with Los Angeles." Other merchants keenly observed the retail experiment, as the potential development of a new shopping district outside the congestion of downtown now appeared to hinge on its failure or success.

In 1928, the total investment in new property on Wilshire Boulevard was estimated at $6,500,000, and that number was projected to skyrocket to approximately fifty million dollars in a single year. Ranch and prairie land, once the home of Major Henry Hancock, John C. Plummer, and other pioneers, sites on Wilshire Boulevard were now among the most desirable real estate in the city. Even before a single customer walked through the doors of the new Bullock's, the gamble appeared to be paying off as a host of businesses announced they would be acquiring a Wilshire Boulevard address. The result? The price of land continued to skyrocket.

HOLLYWOOD BY DESIGN

When Bullock's Wilshire opened, not only was it a huge hit with architecture critics, it also became a popular destination for Hollywood's fashion-conscious celebrities. The most famous of stars, including Greta Garbo, Gloria Swanson, Alfred Hitchcock, Ingrid Bergman, and Katharine Hepburn were all spotted shopping in the store. A young John Wayne was a regular at the Tea Room. Mae West famously preferred to wait in the privacy of her automobile as sales staff would bring a selection of clothes for her to choose from while parked in the motor court.

Some celebrities began their early careers working at Bullock's Wilshire. Actresses Angela Lansbury and June Lockhart were young sales clerks, as was former First Lady Patricia Nixon. Lansbury was hired as a cashier in December of 1942 in anticipation of a busy Christmas season.

"I originally went to Bullock's to get a sort of temporary job, my family—my mother and my twin brothers—we needed the money desperately," she remembers. "It was a very exciting place to work because it really was the crème de la crème of big shops in Los Angeles. There was Bullock's, and there was Bullock's Wilshire."

Lansbury remembers a friendly but very professional

HERMAN SACHS'S *SPIRIT OF TRANSPORTATION* MURAL DEFINED THE CEILING OF THE PORTE CORCHERE.

BULLOCK'S WILSHIRE 175

GEORGE STANLEY, WHO DESIGNED THE OSCAR, CREATED THE SCULPTURAL PLAQUE ABOVE THE WILSHIRE ENTRANCE.

BULLOCK'S WILSHIRE STOREFRONT

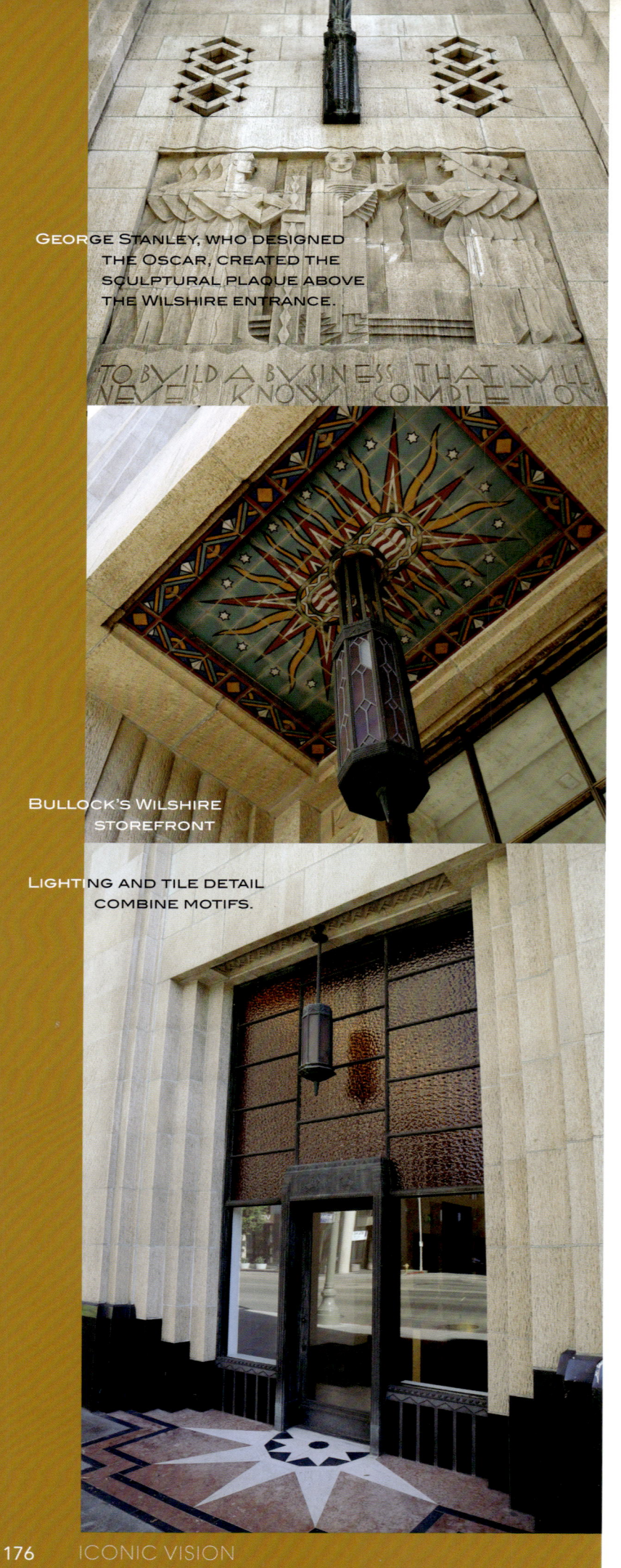

LIGHTING AND TILE DETAIL COMBINE MOTIFS.

atmosphere. "You wore a black dress, and you didn't just hang around. You were an employee, and you minded your business, and you did your job, and you did your best to get on with the saleswomen as they could be very difficult if you kept a client waiting."

"They'd have models walking through the shop, through all the departments looking absolutely glorious in all kinds of gowns, evening gowns, and suits. They were a terrifically nice bunch of women actually, and of course the clientele loved that, being able to stand and look at a beautiful young woman in an outfit and decide whether they could wear that, or their daughter could wear it."

After Christmas, she was invited to return and work as a salesclerk. Because of her "very nice English complexion," she was relocated to the cosmetics department and later sold handbags. She remembers encountering the occasional celebrity. "I saw some great ladies of the screen like Irene Dunn and Ginger Rogers and Marion Davies, the lady friend of William Randolph Hearst who was the great newspaper publisher of the *Los Angeles Examiner*—even in those days he was a legend. I remember Marion Davies walking in with a mink coat dragging along the floor. I was terribly impressed by that."

Lansbury left Bullock's in June of 1943, following a successful MGM screen test. She quickly made her mark on Hollywood, earning an Oscar nomination for Best Supporting Actress for her first movie, *Gaslight*. Creating Lansbury's costumes for the film was designer, Irene Lentz, who had operated Irene's Salon on the second floor of Bullock's Wilshire until 1942. They would work together again on *The Picture of Dorian Gray*, which earned Lansbury a second Best Supporting Actress nomination. Now a successful actress, Lansbury often returned to Bullock's Wilshire, including a memorable shopping trip in 1945 when she purchased a tweed suit that she wore for her wedding to actor, Richard Cromwell. Bullock's Wilshire also served as a filming location for two episodes of *Murder, She Wrote*, her popular TV series.

A number of Hollywood productions have been shot inside Bullock's Wilshire including the film, *Bugsy*, starring Warren Beatty and Annette Bening; *Rough Magic* starring Bridget Fonda, and Aerosmith's *Love In An Elevator* music video.

END OF AN ERA

As the development of Los Angeles continued ever westward, Bullock's Wilshire slipped into a gradual decline. Since the 1940s, it changed ownership twice, first when Bullocks Inc. merged with I. Magnin & Co. and later when Macy's took over, but the Art Deco landmark always retained its original name. The building suffered considerable damage during the 1992 Los Angeles civil uprising

176   ICONIC VISION

The Sportswear department is dominated by artist Gjura Sojano's mural The Spirit of Sports.

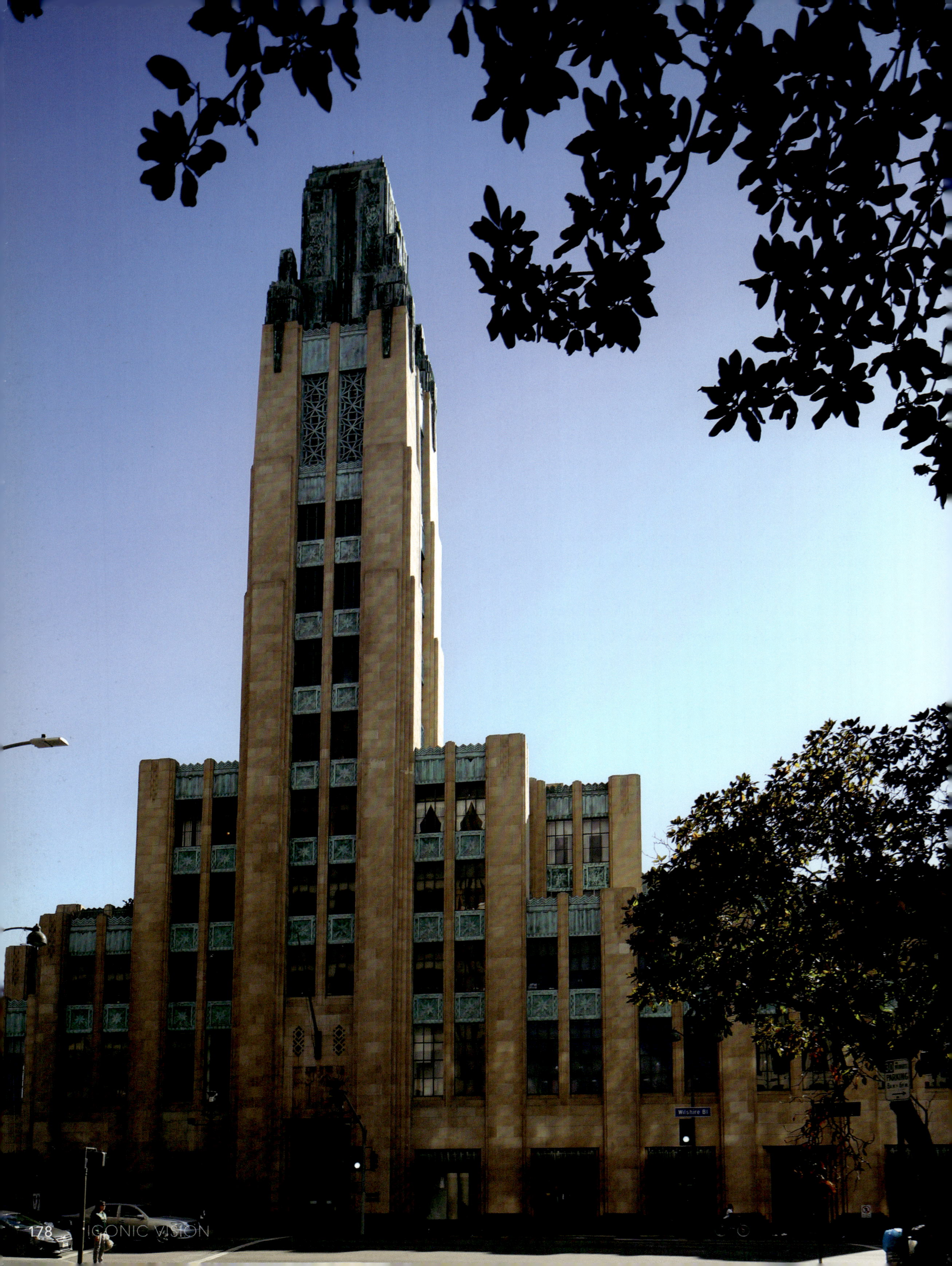
Wilshire Bl

when looters broke in and destroyed display cases. The damage could have been much worse had the staff not shut off the elevators. By April of the following year, the store's retail run had come to an end, as Bullock's Wilshire bid a final farewell to shoppers and closed its doors for good. New life would surface in 1994 when the building was purchased by the Southwestern Law School. The task of converting the once-proud retail giant into an academic institution was assigned to architect Ronald A. Altoon of the architectural firm, Altoon & Porter.

Altoon had first visited Bullock's Wilshire as a five-year-old schoolboy with his mother whom he accompanied when she attended fashion shows or met friends in the tearoom. "It's a soaring building; it lifts the spirits," he explains. "It draws your eye up to the sky and up to the top of the tower. It is a building that is very uplifting and inspiring. It intrigues you to come and see then what is on the inside."

Its years as a glamorous shopping destination were over, but under a new owner, Bullock's Wilshire was about to get a new start housing classrooms, offices, and a law library.

The artwork originally created to entice shoppers now inspires students and faculty, and space is taken up by volumes of important legal works and textbooks.

The Parkinsons' Art Deco masterpiece is included on the National Register of Historic Places and still retains many of the artistic touches that have made it one of Los Angeles's most beloved iconic structures.

AN ADVERTISEMENT HIGHLIGHTS THE STORE BY NIGHT.

A MELANGE OF INTRICATE PATTERNING DEFINES THE EXTERIOR.

Crowds gather for the opening day celebration

OPENING DAY

No transportation project in the history of Los Angeles was contested more bitterly or took longer to navigate through the courts than the Los Angeles Union Passenger Terminal. By the time the legal arguments ended and the first trains arrived, the great dominance of the railroads was coming to an end, and a new era of transcontinental air travel was emerging. The depot would be "the last great train station built anywhere in the world," as architectural historian Thomas S. Hines points out.

Later renamed the Los Angeles Union Station, it was the most recent in a long list of iconic landmarks designed by John Parkinson's firm, and it would be his final architectural contribution. When the station finally opened, the city celebrated with unprecedented pageantry witnessed by more than a half-million people. Long before the sun came up on the morning of May 3, 1939, an excited crowd gathered at the terminal's main entrance on Alameda Street eager to secure a good view of the "Railroads Build the Nation" parade.

The festivities, due to begin at eleven o'clock, were delayed as police and Boy Scout troops struggled to prevent spectators from spilling onto the parade route. On that spring day, the temperature soared, more than twenty people collapsed, and an urgent request went out for additional police officers and squad cars.

The theme of the celebration was transportation, and how it had evolved while Los Angeles, itself, was evolving into a major metropolis. Commencing at Eighth and Alameda streets, ox-drawn carts, stagecoaches, and automobiles shared the route with the "streamlined juggernauts of steel" that now sped across the nation's railroad network. "Cheers and laughter mingled in a gay cacophony as a cavalcade of the nation's transportation wheeled and marched through the banked throngs," the *Los Angeles Examiner* reported.

Leading the parade were the massed colors of the American Legion, followed by members of the Los Angeles City Council, Mayor Fletcher Bowron, and California Governor Culbert Olson in their respective automobiles. Los Angeles County Sheriff Eugene W. Biscailuz served as grand marshal, riding proudly on a gleaming silver saddle atop his white horse.

As an enormous railway gun, normally kept at Fort MacArthur, came into view, the crowd gasping in awe of such a sight. Parade viewers applauded the trucks of the 63rd Coast Artillery and their new anti-aircraft guns and looked on nostalgically as the oldest steam engine in California, the Collis P. Huntington, passed by.

Before the last floats even reached the reviewing stand, officials went ahead and began the dedication ceremony to make up for all the delays. When the city's leading lawyer and chairman of the terminal's opening-day celebration committee, Henry W. O'Melveny, took to the podium, the sound of his voice booming over the loudspeakers sparked the immense crowd to push closer toward the stage. After an appeal for calm and a short speech from Governor Olson, Mayor Bowron officially accepted the station on behalf of the city.

The theme of the Opening Day parade was "Railroads Build the Nation."

Los Angeles Union Passenger Terminal Opening Day celebrations

"Our hopes are more than fulfilled," as the *Examiner* reported that day, Mayor Bowron told the crowd. "Our expectations are completely realized in this beautiful station. It will fill the transportation needs of Los Angeles for generations to come. I speak for the people of Los Angeles when I offer my thanks to the presidents of the railroads for the magnificent terminal. Los Angeles is indeed proud."

At the conclusion of the dedication, a three-hundred-piece band performed "The Star-Spangled Banner" in a ceremony jointly conducted by the Native Sons and Daughters of the Golden West and a company of the 160th Infantry. It was late afternoon by the time the public was allowed inside to witness the majesty of the city's brand new train station designed by John and Donald Parkinson.

That evening, more than 1,200 civic leaders joined the heads of the three major railroads at a lavish banquet at the Biltmore Hotel. In their after-dinner speeches, Angus D. McDonald, the tall and white-haired chief of the Southern Pacific, Edward M. Engel, the head of the Santa Fe, and William M. Jeffers, president of Union Pacific, proclaimed a sense of unity and purpose with Los Angeles city leaders that a decade earlier would have been entirely unimaginable.

A BITTER FIGHT

The rivaling Union Pacific, Southern Pacific, and Atchison, Topeka & Santa Fe railroads fought the concept of a shared Los Angeles depot with such fervor, one of their attorneys declared they were "training their children to carry on the opposition after them." Not only did the city and the railroads bicker over the need for the station and who should pay for it, they also squabbled over its location. While city politicians wanted it located in the heart of Chinatown, the railroads put forth a series of alternatives, including expanding the existing Southern Pacific Central Station John Parkinson designed at Fifth Street and Central Avenue.

Unable to agree on a single substantive point, the railroads waged a fierce battle that would last a generation. As early as 1905, a Los Angeles Chamber of Commerce committee was set up to explore the benefits of a union station, but the idea was quickly abandoned in the face of determined opposition from the railroads. Between 1900 and 1910, the population of the city grew by 211% to 319,198, and the need to safely separate the public and the railroads forced civic leaders to examine ways of eliminating grade crossings, blamed for numerous traffic accidents and increasing congestion.

The city's transport problems led to the hiring of Bion J. Arnold, who helped develop New York City's Interborough Rapid

SOUTHERN PACIFIC'S LOS ANGELES CENTRAL STATION, DESIGNED BY PARKINSON, OPENED IN 1914.

THE PARKINSONS' $400,000 UNION STATION IN OGDEN, UTAH, 1922

UNION PACIFIC DEPOT, CALIENTE, NEVADA

UNION STATION   183

Transit subway system. The Los Angeles City Council requested that he come up with ideas for a more efficient system. In 1911, Arnold examined the feasibility of building a union station that would combine scattered railroad facilities, and his report recommended locating such a depot on a site adjacent to the original Plaza site in the heart of the city, where it ultimately would be built.

However, persuading the railroads to support the project appeared impossible, and a showdown with the city became inevitable. In 1916, the Civic Center Association and several other local groups filed a complaint with the California Railroad Commission, urging the body to address the city's grade-crossing problem and work toward a union station. The railroads opposed the petition, and the following year, when the Commission failed to resolve the issue, it was taken up by the California Supreme Court, which ultimately ruled a shared terminal should be built.

In the months that ensued, both sides fought in numerous hearings until 1921 when the California Railroad Commission ordered the station to be constructed. The following year, the railroads appealed the commission's decision before the California Supreme Court, which struck down the commission's order. The case went all the way to the United States Supreme Court, which ultimately supported the California Supreme Court's decision, and the railroads prevailed.

Frustrated, the city switched tactics and petitioned the Interstate Commerce Commission (ICC), a government agency overseeing various aspects of the operation of the railroads. In July of 1925, after a lengthy investigation, the ICC determined the terminal was needed and should be built.

As the two sides battled to an apparent standstill, the railroads offered the city an alternative that would remove scores of interurban trains from crowded Los Angeles streets. Instead of building a union station, they proposed linking their existing terminals with a series of elevated tracks, creating a "virtual union station." The railroads proposed allowing the Pacific Electric full access to the new lines. City engineers scoffed at the offer, arguing elevated railroads were both unsightly and unsafe, and the railroads fired back, insisting a union station would only add to the city's congestion woes.

In an attempt to settle the long dispute once and for all, two propositions appeared on the ballot as voters went to the polls in April

DONALD PARKINSON, LEFT, AND HIS FATHER JOHN PUT THE FINAL TOUCHES ON PRELIMINARY SKETCHES FOR A NEW $11 MILLION LOS ANGELES UNION PASSENGER TERMINAL IN JANUARY 1934.

The railroads' architectural committee pressed for a design inspired by the Santa Barbara County Courthouse.

THE PARKINSONS PROPOSED FOUR DESIGNS FOR THE LOS ANGELES UNION PASSENGER TERMINAL. SCHEME "C" WAS FAVORED EARLY ON BY THE RAILROADS AS IT WAS "BETTER SUITED FOR LOS ANGELES THAN THE CONVENTIONAL TYPE OF STATION" DUE TO ITS SPANISH STYLE.

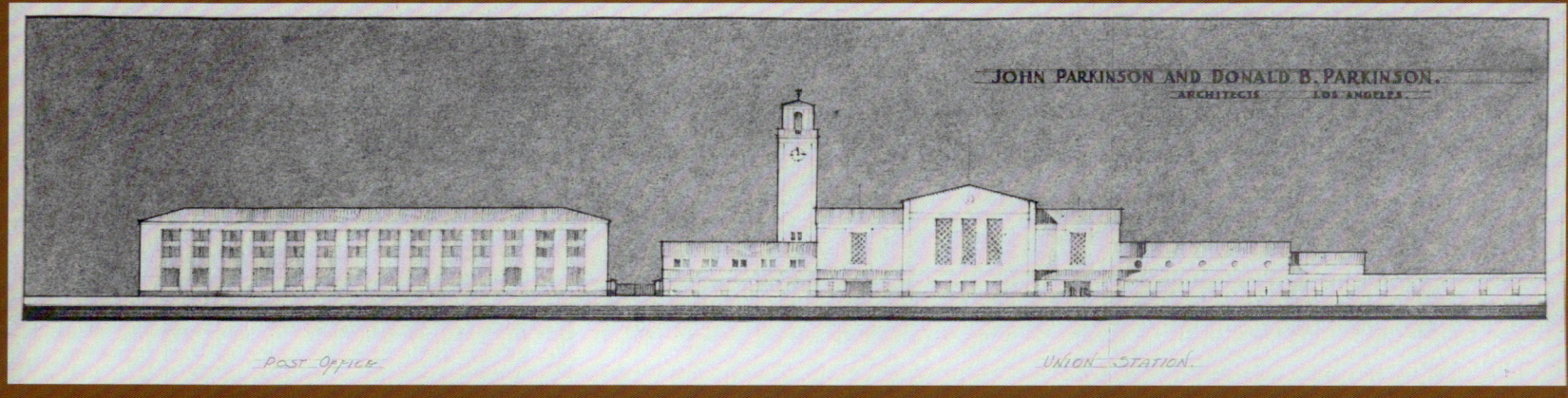

IN 1935, THE U.S. POST OFFICE ANNOUNCED PLANS FOR A TERMINAL ANNEX NEAR THE NEW STATION. THE RAILROADS FEARED THE STRUCTURE WOULD DWARF THEIR NEW DEPOT, SO THE PARKINSONS RENDERED A NEW DRAWING TO SHOW THE SCALE.

MURALISTS COMPETED TO DECORATE THE EAST WALL OF THE LOS ANGELES UNION PASSENGER TERMINAL WAITING ROOM. HUGO BALLIN, WHO HAD CREATED WORKS FOR THE TITLE INSURANCE AND TITLE GUARANTEE BUILDINGS SUBMITTED TWO DESIGNS; NO MURAL WAS USED IN THE FINAL DESIGN.

LOS ANGELES UNION
PASSENGER TERMINAL,
UNDER CONSTRUCTION

of 1926. Los Angeles residents were asked first, if a union station should be built in the city, and second, whether such a station should be located near the Plaza. To win public support for their "no" vote campaign, the railroads launched an aggressive public-relations blitz, utilizing billboards, house-to-house canvassing, and costly newspaper advertisements. "Los Angeles has been literally flooded with propaganda signed by organizations which are transparent dummies for the railroads," the *Los Angeles Times* reported days before the election.

"The destiny of Los Angeles does not hang upon a union station," William Sproule, president of the Southern Pacific Company, argued in a campaign advertisement published in the *Times*. "The Southern Pacific and the Union Pacific have great and lasting interest in having suitable terminal facilities, and the traveling public approve the present Central Passenger Terminal."

City Attorney Jess E. Stephens argued the city's case in a series of public meetings, warning voters the railroads would "resort to any desperate means to arouse prejudice in the minds of voters."

When the ballots were counted on April 30, 1926, the "yes" campaign prevailed on both measures, although the margin of victory was slim on the second proposition dealing with the station's proposed Plaza location.

The following year, the California Railroad Commission determined for a second time that a union station should be built, and in May of 1928, the ICC approved the decision. Digging in their heels once more, the railroads put in motion yet-another appeals process, arguing before the California Supreme Court that the California Railroad Commission's 1927 order lacked the proper authority.

The order was upheld, however, by the state's high court in May of 1930, and again, the railroads refused to relinquish. Following a familiar path, the matter was taken up once more by the United States Supreme Court, which ultimately upheld the California ruling. "It is plain that this is a great victory for the city and its need for union passenger facilities. This decision clears up the last bit of pending litigation," a relieved City Attorney Erwin P. Werner told the *Los Angeles Times*.

Soon after, the Great Depression had fallen upon the country, and the number of passengers traveling by rail plummeted. In October of 1932, the railroads asked for a moratorium on the project, but the city not only rejected the request, but also turned down a subsequent proposal to build a cheaper terminal on North Broadway. By way of a compromise, the city offered to put up one million dollars to pay for the preliminary street work.

By 1933, after years of wrangling and faced with a long list of legal rulings against them, the presidents of the three railroads finally conceded, announcing in a statement they would begin building a shared terminal. The estimated cost of the new train station was nine million dollars.

UNION STATION

LOS ANGELES UNION PASSENGER TERMINAL

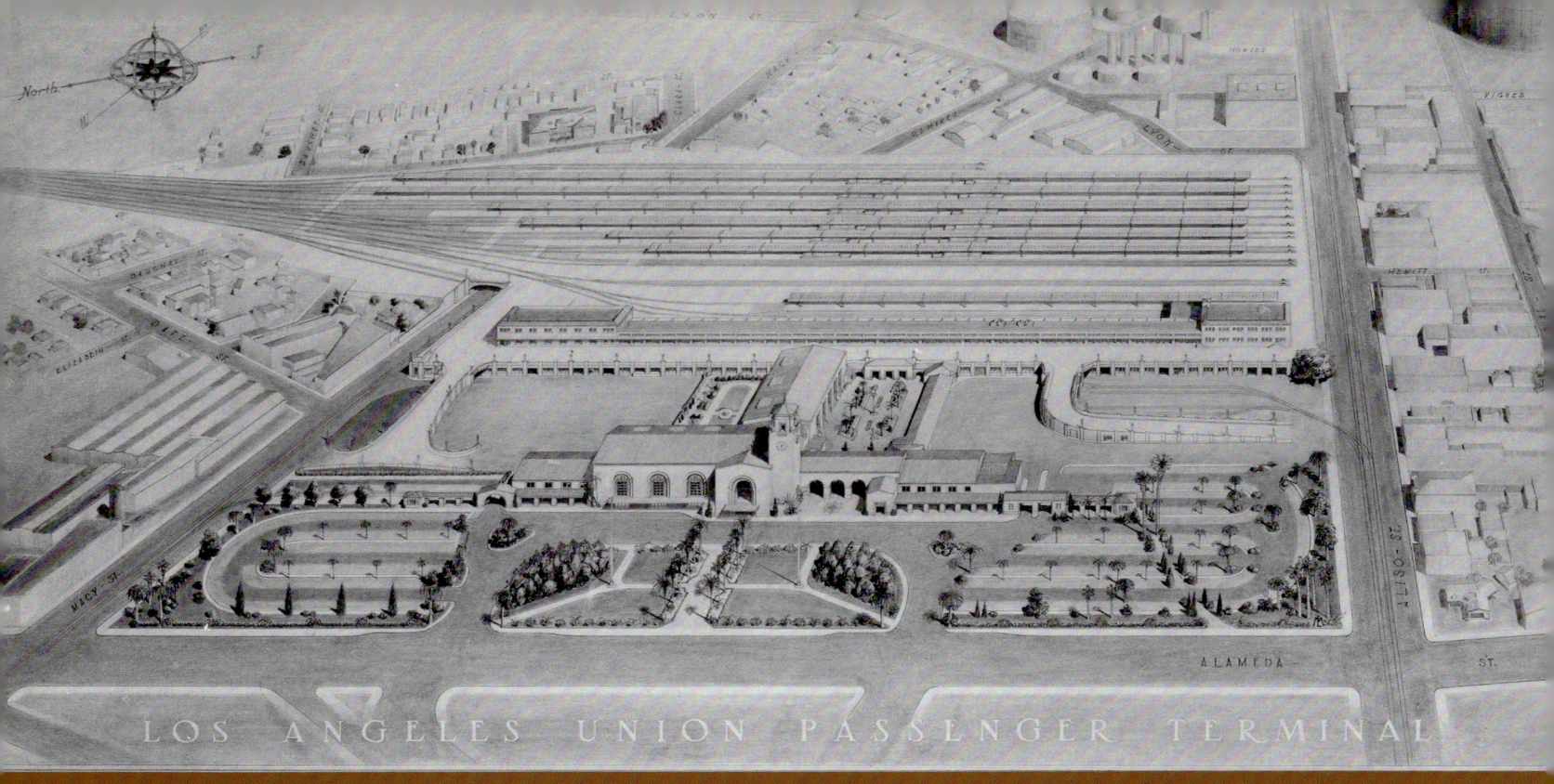

THE CITY FAVORED THE PLAZA SITE, BETWEEN MACY AND ALISO STREETS, AS IT WAS CLOSE TO THE AREA WHERE THE THREE RAILROADS ENTERED THE CITY. TO BUILD A UNION STATION THERE MEANT THE OLD CHINATOWN WOULD HAVE TO BE DEMOLISHED, AN ENTIRE COMMUNITY WOULD BE UPROOTED, AND THE HISTORIC CENTER OF CHINESE AMERICAN LIFE WOULD BE DESTROYED.

A FINAL LANDMARK

John Parkinson's experience designing the Southern Pacific's Central Station as well as railroad depots as far away as Caliente, Nevada, and Ogden, Utah, made his firm the obvious choice to create a new union station in Los Angeles. On November 10, 1933, John and Donald Parkinson submitted a bid for the work, and a month later, they were hired as consulting architects. The Parkinsons would maintain a close but often strained working relationship with the chief architects of the three railroads, H.L. Gilman (Santa Fe), J.H. Christie (Southern Pacific) and R.J. Wirth (Union Pacific).

Work on the station's design began early the next year when John and Donald Parkinson welcomed the Architectural Committee of the Los Angeles Union Passenger Terminal (LAUPT) to their offices in the Title Insurance Building. John Parkinson began the meeting by stressing the importance of a design that would complement that of City Hall. However, the railroads made it clear they favored an informal "California-style structure" similar to the courthouse in Santa Barbara.

The Parkinsons agreed to make studies of four distinct architectural styles and to submit preliminary plans. After reviewing the options, the railroads agreed on a Spanish-style structure that would be "radically different from the usual type of union station." John and Donald Parkinson estimated it would take them eight months to prepare the final plans.

"The reported decision of the three railroads concerned to build the new union station at the Plaza in the California-style of architecture is a wise one," the *Los Angeles Times* wrote in an editorial in August of 1934. "A contrast between the rather monumental buildings now in the Civic Center, and the low rambling structure typical of this locality—whether it is called Californian, Spanish Mission, Mexican, Mediterranean, or Moorish—should be pleasing, always providing it is well drawn and executed."

The *Los Angeles Daily News* was equally positive; "The decision of the railroads to build their union station in the Old California-Spanish manner will bring hearty plaudits from those who for years have tried to introduce in downtown Los Angeles a distinctive architectural note."

The project now underway, John Parkinson met early on with the heads of the various railroads and their common architectural committee, while leaving the day-to-day meetings to his son. In May, confident everything was under control, he headed to Colon, Panama, with his wife on vacation. They also traveled by sea to Gibraltar, then to Genoa, Italy, where they embarked on a road trip through Austria, Germany, and Holland, eventually sailing to England before returning to the United States.

Once back in Los Angeles, Parkinson found the railroads were growing increasingly frustrated with the escalating cost of the firm's

Artist Herman Sachs inspects the tile work inside the Los Angeles Union Passenger Terminal. Donald Parkinson lobbied the railroads to hire Sachs as a color consultant and designer for the project after working with him on the Title Insurance Building and Los Angeles City Hall.

UNION STATION 189

Union Station Entrance

Union Station Clock

Union Station Interior

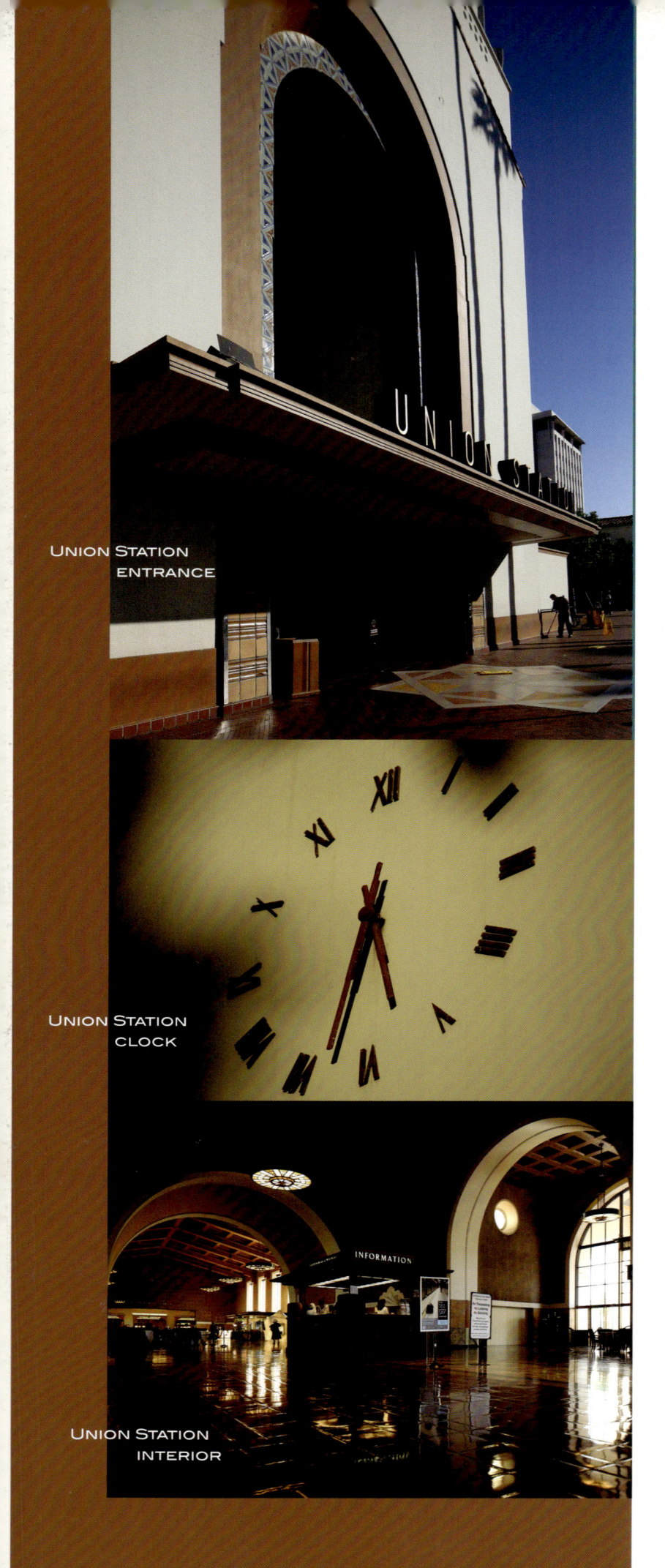

ambitious plans. Of particular concern was the vast amount of marble wainscoting and terra cotta walls proposed for the waiting room and the use of black and colored granite as a base for the front elevation.

"You will observe that the Architectural Committee has observed that Parkinson & Parkinson are treating the plans in a more elaborate manner than is justified," M.C. Blanchard, chief engineer of the LAUPT, wrote to the chief engineers at Southern Pacific and Union Pacific. John and Donald Parkinson were warned if their plans did not conform to the budget, the railroads' architectural committee would consider hiring a chief draftsman to create an alternative plan that would.

Los Angeles Mayor Frank L. Shaw was also critical of the Parkinsons' plans, but for different reasons. He reportedly "took vigorous exception to the Parkinson architectural plan, stating that he expected a more imposing and magnificent station, comparing favorably with the Kansas City and Washington stations."

As concerns over the cost of the Parkinsons' plans grew, the architectural committee took the bold step of producing its own plan for the union depot and submitted a copy to John and Donald Parkinson for their review. The elder Parkinson was clearly annoyed by the insult, but responded in typically controlled fashion. "In our opinion, the architectural forms used in the design submitted to us, have been poorly chosen as to character, and they lack the enduring quality which must exist in such a building as the Union Passenger Terminal, representing three great Railway Companies and used by millions of people in all walks of life over a period of many years," he wrote. "This criticism in particular, applies to the shape of the major openings in the building and the complicated forms of the tower. The forms in question might be highly appropriate for a Mexican amusement center such as Agua Caliente, or for the exotic Exposition group built in San Diego in 1915, but not for the building in question." Parkinson included a revised design with his reply.

Less than a month after penning his response, John Parkinson died at his Santa Monica home. News of his passing reached the railroad bosses by way of telegram on December 11. "John Parkinson, senior member of the firm, passed away Dec. 9th, buried 10th. Donald, son and junior member, will carry on the business. Donald has been only active member on LAUPT work and will continue as consultant. Terminal forces will make detail design. City has approved plan and elevation." (The telegram has been preserved in the Los Angeles Union Station Collection in the USC Libraries Special Collections.)

While his father's sudden and unexpected death came as a shock, Donald Parkinson was already well-positioned to assume full

Union Station

UNION STATION
TICKET HALL

control of the architectural firm. In the coming months, he would guide the project through a seemingly endless series of revisions, while carrying the added burden of making sure the train station was a fitting final tribute to his father's immense architectural legacy.

STATION DESIGN

In the spring of 1939, the Los Angeles Union Passenger Terminal was finally finished at an estimated cost of eleven million dollars. To keep costs from escalating, Donald Parkinson was forced to compromise and give up a number of colorful embellishments including plans for an elaborate mural on the east wall of the waiting room.

The building was widely praised by critics who marveled how the architects managed to combine the charm of days gone by with dynamic twentieth-century style. The *Los Angeles Evening Herald and Express* declared the new station, "a milestone of progress in the city's history." And the *California Arts & Architecture* magazine raved, "There may be bigger railroad stations, but there is none more complete, nor as handsome."

The design was widely referred to as "Mission Moderne" by commentators who struggled to find a catchall term to describe the varied architectural styles blended into the structure. The Spanish heritage was most evident in the exterior design, the slanted tile roof, stucco arcades, balconies, and patios. The glamour of Art Deco, so masterfully expressed in Bullock's Wilshire, was on display in the Gothic sign work throughout the terminal, and then there was the rectangular Moorish clock tower rising 125 feet, proudly beckoning travelers to step inside.

As historian Kevin Starr explains, how fitting it was that John Parkinson's final project showcased a combination of architectural styles. "In that last great work, that summarizing work, it was as if he was telling the story of his whole architectural experience," he says. "It was as if he was telling the story of Los Angeles, itself, in his time. It is a Spanish building, and it brings up the flavor of the Spanish and Mission era. It is a Moderne building, and it has the mood of the 1920s, the Streamline quality of the 1930s. It has got an Art Deco, festive quality to it."

The layout of the forty-five-acre site was divided into three distinct sections. First, the main passenger station buildings were set back approximately two hundred feet from Alameda Street and measured 850 feet in length. Next, the mail, baggage, and express building stretched 1,200 feet, located behind the main terminal buildings. Finally, the third section was made up of the tracks and train sheds on the grounds.

A tunnel provided access to the train concourse: sixteen

Union Station waiting room

UNION STATION 193

Union Station
Exterior

passenger tracks with a capacity of twelve to twenty coaches each. There were eight tracks to handle mail, baggage, and express, five tracks for private cars, plus three more engine-release tracks—six for switching and one for storage. Sixty trains and seven thousand passengers were expected daily. Eight additional trains would run twice a week.

The principal entrance to the main white concrete building was through a fifty-foot arched opening, bordered with mosaic tile in different shades of blue, gray-green and burnt sienna. Once inside, visitors were greeted by vast halls with arched ceilings featuring concrete-encased steel ridge beams and rafters painted by Herman Sachs to resemble a Spanish mission. Underfoot, floor mosaics made of marble from Vermont, Tennessee, Belgium, France, and Spain gave the appearance of vast carpets.

In the ticket hall, imposing arched windows lined two of the four sides, allowing ample light to flood the 115-foot-long, 25-foot-deep American black walnut ticket counter that stood against the east wall, ready to do business. Officials at the three main railroads drew straws to decide who occupied the different positions at the ticket counter. The vast windows in both the ticket concourse and waiting room were fitted with amber cathedral glass to soften the glare of the afternoon sun.

The wainscoting on the walls of the ticket concourse and the waiting room had a six-inch base of Belgian black marble surmounted by a three-foot-high geometric tile design created by Gladding, McBean & Co. Capping this was a two-inch band of Campan Melange marble, followed by Montana Sienna travertine decorated with three-inch decorative tile inserts and an eight-inch band of painted hard plaster.

Stretching to the ceiling was a newly developed acoustical tile that helped make station announcements more audible and reduced ambient noise. Both rooms boasted a series of ornamental chandeliers, each ten feet in diameter and weighing more than three thousand pounds. The waiting room featured comfortable, oversized Art Deco leather armchairs. Around the station, metal trim included bronze decoration for doors and windows and wrought-iron grilles.

Adjacent to the waiting room, the south patio offered travelers a place to escape into a well-manicured garden that included olive, pepper, and palm trees bordered with carefully trimmed hedges, while the landscaped north patio provided an ideal area for outdoor dining. The train concourse, the arrival/departure lobby, and reception hall featured geometric tile patterns on the wainscoting, while the floors were laid with Spanish tiles.

Coin-operated showers were installed in the washrooms for passengers, and a four-chair barbershop was onsite, should a new haircut be required. Visitors could also savor a meal in the Fred Harvey Company restaurant and cocktail lounge, designed by Mary Colter in a nineteenth-century Spanish Provincial style. A striking red, black, and buff Valencia Spanish Cement tile floor welcomed guests into the main dining room where there was seating for twenty-seven people at a U-shaped counter and two hundred in the tables and booths. The adjoining cocktail lounge featured a bar and twelve private booths.

"There may be larger terminals in many of the metropolitan cities of the east and Midwest, but none more modern or better planned, and none so beautiful and glamorous," *Architect and Engineer* proclaimed in its May 1939 edition. *Southwest Builder and Contractor* even predicted, "in all the world it has no counterpart and as an expression of Southern California spirit and architecture, it is destined to spread the fame of Los Angeles already known for its many wonderful places."

Nearly a half-century after he first arrived in Los Angeles, John Parkinson's final contribution was at last unveiled. Union Station endures, and remains one of the busiest and most beloved architectural icons in Los Angeles.

JOHN PARKINSON,
Architect.

ACKNOWLEDGMENTS

THIS BOOK WAS BROUGHT TO LIFE THROUGH THE EFFORTS OF MANY PEOPLE. I acknowledge the gracious support of Wm. Scott Field, owner of the Parkinson Archives. I thank Paddy Calistro and Scott McAuley of Angel City Press for their incredible passion for this book, and Hilary Lentini, Leanna Hanson, and Alan Altur of Lentini Design for the distinctive graphic design. I also thank Lynn Relfe, Kathy McGuire, Jed Smith, and Niree Perian of Angel City Press for their editorial support.

I am grateful to Sandra Stojanovic for all the wonderful original photographs of modern-day Los Angeles, which complement the timeless elegance of Parkinson's buildings and demonstrate Sandra's keen eye for historical significance and detail. I also thank all of John Parkinson's relatives who aided in the research, including Kimberley P. DeCambre, Melanie Parkinson Larson, Pamela Parkinson Kellogg, Anna Trent Moore, Cathy Harris-Gorzadek, Thea Zuliani, Melissa McCollister, and Judy Gumaer Testa. I would like to thank Anne Neblett and her daughter Nancy Neblett Medlin, and I express my sincere appreciation to the many experts who were interviewed for the documentary that inspired this book, including Kevin Starr, William Deverell, Thomas S. Hines, Jeffrey K. Ochsner, Kenneth Briesch, and Ronald A. Altoon, as well as Angela Lansbury.

I thank Jon Lee at the Coliseum for allowing me to explore a truly iconic structure, Jeff Cooper for the same privilege at Union Station, and Debbie Leathers at the Southwestern Law School. I thank the staff of the Los Angeles Public Library, especially Christina Rice, for helping to find fantastic images to illustrate this story, as well as John Cahoon, collections manager at the Seaver Center for Western History Research, and also the staff at the University of Washington Libraries Special Collections. Kathleen Correia, supervising librarian at the California State Library, was a great help, as was the staff of the Napa Historical Society, Huntington Library, UCLA Library Special Collections, and the Getty Research Institute. Dace Taube and Rachelle Balinas Smith at USC Libraries Special Collections helped identify incredible images, as did Josef K. Lesser at the Los Angeles Railroad Heritage Foundation. Lee Witten of the Ogden Union Station Collection, and David Kernberger of Historic Photos, also deserve special thanks.

I thank John and Christine Ackers, Tom Pridmore, and the Rev. David Brown for helping me research John Parkinson's life in Scorton. I thank my parents Dorothy and Harry Gee for sharing in the adventure of researching this story. I would like to say a special thank-you to Christina Chan, Martha Sanchez-Avila, Dena Flekman, Bev Meyer, Ron Garcia, Peyton McElyea, Caliente Mayor Keith Larson, Captain Larry Schneider, Angela Chan, Daniel Brown, David Trilling, Ron Johnson, Susan Kwan, and Jo, whose efforts made the words in this book so much more meaningful.

I would also like to thank the many other people who have supported this project, including Bob Peirce, Sharon Harroun Peirce, Lauren Stone, Georgina Charles, Kamilla Blanche, Lisa Schechter, Bret Parsons, Tom Zimmerman and especially the always-enthusiastic Councilmember Tom LaBonge, who shares my fascination with the world John Parkinson created in Los Angeles.

Researching John Parkinson's story has been an enormous privilege, and I am profoundly grateful for the experience.

—Stephen Gee

Donald B. Parkinson, Watercolor

PHOTO CREDITS

Except as detailed below, the images showcased on the pages of *Iconic Vision* are from the author's personal collection. Every effort has been made to determine the origins of vintage photographs and give appropriate credit to its source. Any oversights will be corrected in future editions.

The Parkinson Archives, courtesy of Wm. Scott Field, owner: 10, 12, 72, 87, 102, 104 (middle upper), 107 (top), 108, 110 (top), 114, 125 (top and middle), 135, 141, 156, 157 (top), 160 (middle), 168, 170 (top).

J.S. and L.M.C. Ackers: 23.

California State Library: 28-29, 58, 81, 95, 104 (top); Mott-Merge Collection: 14 (middle lower), 112, 115 (top and middle), 119, 132, 133 (middle lower), 154 (bottom), 157 (bottom), 164, 170 (middle), 171, 172, 174, 177; Mushet Photography: 117, 118.

Kimberly P. DeCambre: 21.

Fairfax High School: 111.

Fresno County Public Library: 35.

Cathy Harris-Gorzadek: 59 (top), 198.

Historic Photos, St. Helena, California: 32-33.

Huntington Library: 166, 167.

International Newsreel/SG: 146 (top), 151.

Pamela Parkinson Kellogg: 97, 116 (top), 144.

Melanie Parkinson Larson: 109, 110 (bottom).

Library of Congress: 142-143, 150 (middle upper).

L.A. Public Library Photos: 13, 57 (top), 80 (top), 122, 130 (middle), 146 (bottom), 148, 150 (bottom), 152-153, 159, 189.

L.A. Railroad Heritage Foundation Collection, by Ralph Melching: 187; Marc Wanamaker Collection: 183 (top).

Minnesota Historical Society: 26, 27.

Napa Historical Society: 30.

Anne Neblett: 79.

Ogden Union Station Collection: 183 (middle).

Captain Larry Schneider: 67.

Seaver Center for Western History Research, Los Angeles County Museum of Natural History: 8, 80 (bottom), 161 (middle).

Sandra Stojanovic: 2, 6, 14 (middle upper, bottom), 15 (bottom), 16, 17 (top), 55, 63 (bottom), 64 (middle), 68 (top), 69, 70 (top), 71, 76, 84, 88-89, 90 (bottom), 92 (bottom), 98 (top, middle lower, bottom), 99, 103 (bottom), 104 (middle upper, bottom), 105, 106, 107 (bottom), 115 (bottom), 116 (bottom), 120, 121, 123, 124, 125 (bottom), 129, 134 (bottom), 138, 139, 145, 160 (bottom), 161 (top and bottom), 162, 163, 169 (top), 178, 179 (bottom), 181, 183 (bottom), 185, 190, 193, 194.

U.S. Patent Office: 63 (top).

UCLA Charles E. Young Research Library, Department of Special Collections: John C. Austin Papers, 4; *Los Angeles Times* Photographic Archives: 147, 182 (top).

Union Pacific Museum: 180, 182 (bottom).

University of Southern California, USC Libraries Special Collections: 15, 17 (bottom), 60-61, 100-101, 103 (top), 128, 130 (top), 146 (middle), 150 (top), 154 (top), 186; Parkinson Archives: 186, 188.

University of Washington Libraries, Special Collections Division: Boyd and Brass: 38 (bottom); Asahel Curtis: 41, 48 (middle upper, middle lower), 51 (top, bottom); Frank La Roche: 46; Washington Localities: 43, 48 (bottom).

Thea Zuliani: 50 (top).

Tom Zimmerman: back cover

The images on pages 18, 20, 23, 24, 25, 34 (top), 42 (top), and 54 were published in *Incidents by the Way: The Boy! What Has the Future in Store for Him? What Will Be His Experience?* by John Parkinson. Los Angeles: Press of G. Rice & Sons, 1935.

The image on page 36 was published in *American Architect and Building News*.

The image on page 196 was published in *As We See 'Em, a Volume of Cartoons and Caricatures of Los Angeles Citizens* by Antony E. Anderson. Los Angeles: E. A. Thomson, 1900.

The images on pages 56 (bottom), 74 (top), and 136 (top) were published in *Greater Los Angeles and Southern California, Portraits and Personal Memoranda* by Robert J. Burdette. Chicago: Lewis, 1910.

The images on pages 64 (bottom), 78, 90 (top), 91 (bottom), 92 (top), 93 (top, bottom), 94 (middle), 96, and 203 were published in *John Parkinson and Donald B. Parkinson, Architects*. Publisher: Denny A. Clark (1921)

The images on pages 56 (top), 62, 66, 68 (bottom), 70, 73 (top, middle), 74 (middle), 77 (bottom), and 184 were published in *Our Architecture: Morgan & Walls, John Parkinson, Hunt & Eager, Los Angeles, California, 1904*, by John L. LeBerthon. Los Angeles: J.L. LeBerthon, 1904.

The images on pages 64 (top) and 158 were published in *Notables of the West*. New York: International News Service, 1913.

The image on pages 82-83 was published in *The Architect and Engineer of California*. September 1910.

BIBLIOGRAPHY

"The Los Angeles Union Passenger Railway Station." *The Architect and Engineer* 136.

"Los Angeles Union Passenger Terminal." *The Architectural Digest* 10, no. 2 (1939).

"Manual Arts High School." *Architectural Concrete*, November 3, 1936.

McCollister, Melissa. Telephone interview by author. September 25, 2010.

McGroarty, John Steven. *Los Angeles from the Mountains to the Sea: With Selected Biography of Actors and Witnesses to the Period of Growth and Achievement*. Chicago: American Historical Society, 1921.

McMilian, Elizabeth Jean. *Deco & Streamline Architecture in L.A.: A Modern City Survey*. Schiffer Publishing, 2004.

McNichols, Donald. *Seattle Pacific University: A Growing Vision, 1891-1991*. Seattle, WA: University, 1989.

Moore, Anna Trent. Interview by author. October 16, 2010.

Neblett, Anne. Interview by author. July 30, 2011.

"The New City Hall, Los Angeles, California." *American Architect*, April 20, 1927.

Notables of the West. N.Y.: International News Service, 1913.

Ochsner, Jeffrey Karl. Interview by author. October 1, 2011.

—., and Dennis Alan. Andersen. *Distant Corner: Seattle Architects and the Legacy of H.H. Richardson*. Seattle: University of Washington Press, 2003.

—. *Shaping Seattle Architecture: A Historical Guide to the Architects*. Seattle: University of Washington Press in Association with the American Institute of Architects Seattle Chapter and the Seattle Architectural Foundation, 1994.

"Olympic Stadium in Los Angeles." *The Architectural Record* 70 (1931): 419-24.

Pace, Harold. *Vintage American Road Racing Cars 1950-1970*. Motorbooks, 2004.

Parkinson, John. *Incidents by the Way: The Boy! What Has the Future in Store for Him? What Will Be His Experience?*. Los Angeles: Press of G. Rice & Sons, 1935.

Rehart, Catherine Morison. *The Valley's Legends & Legacies*. Fresno, California: Word Dancer Press, 1996.

Reiff, Daniel D. *Houses from Books: Treatises, Pattern Books, and Catalogs in American Architecture, 1738-1950: A History and Guide*. University Park, PA: Pennsylvania State University Press, 2000.

Representative Men of Manitoba: History in Portraiture: A Gallery of Men Whose Energy, Ability, Enterprise and Public Spirit Have Produced the Marvellous Record of the Prairie Province. Winnipeg: Tribune Pub., 1902.

Ring, Frances Kroll. *Champions in the Sun: A Special Issue of* California History, *the Magazine of the California Historical Society*. San Francisco: California Historical Society, 1984.

Schindler, Pauline G. "A Significant Contribution to Culture." *California Arts & Architecture*, January 1930.

"School for Manual Arts." *Architectural Forum* 65 (1936).

Servin, Manuel P., and Iris Higbie Wilson. *Southern California And Its University, A History of USC*. 1969.

Signor, John R. *The Los Angeles and Salt Lake Railroad Company: Union Pacific's Historic Salt Lake Route*. San Marino, California: Golden West Books, 1988.

Starr, Kevin. *Embattled Dreams: California in War and Peace, 1940-1950*. Oxford: Oxford University Press, 2002.

—. Interview by author. September 29, 2010.

BIBLIOGRAPHY

—. *Material Dreams: Southern California through the 1920s*. New York: Oxford University Press, 1990.

Twelve Pioneers of Los Angeles. Los Angeles: Times-Mirror Printing & Binding House, for Its Friends, 1928.

Vandor, Paul E. *History of Fresno County, California, with Biographical Sketches of the Leading Men and Women of the County Who Have Been Identified with Its Growth and Development from the Early Days to the Present*. Los Angeles: Historic Record, 1919.

"Vega Occupying New Factory." *Western Flying*, March 1941.

Warner, George E., C.M. Foote, Edward D. Neill, and J. Fletcher Williams. *History of Hennepin County and the City of Minneapolis including the Explorers and Pioneers of Minnesota*. Minneapolis: North Star Pub., 1881.

Weaver, John D. *El Pueblo Grande, A Non-Fiction Book About Los Angeles*. Los Angeles: Ward Ritchie Press, 1973.

"Western Advertising, John G. Bullock Tells Why It Pays To Spend Millions." *Art in Business*, February 6, 1930.

Winter, Robert, and David Gebhard. *An Architectural Guidebook to Los Angeles*. Salt Lake City: Gibbs Smith, 2003.

Workman, Boyle, and Caroline Walker. *Boyle Workman's The City That Grew*. Los Angeles: Southland Pub., 1936.

JOANNES BROTHERS BUILDING, 1917; HOME TO BEN HUR COFFEE, TEA, AND SPICES

INDEX

Adler, Dankmar 92
Adventures of Superman 14
Agricultural Department 103
Agricultural Park 55, 133, 135
Alexander, Harry L. 80
Alexandria Hotel 13, 80, 87, 90
Allen, Harris 166
Allied Architects Association 94, 154, 155, 157, 158
Allied Architects Association of Los Angeles 94
Altoon & Porter 179
Altoon, Ronald A. 179
American Architect and Building News .. 80
American Bridge Company of Chicago .. 92
American Institute of Architects 94, 120, 154
American Legion 181
Angelus Hotel 77
Architect and Engineer 195, 170, 200
Architectural Forum 109, 120, 200
Arnold, Bion J. 183
Art Deco 13, 14, 113, 120, 165, 169, 170, 176, 179, 192, 195
Associated Press 64
Atchison, Topeka & Santa Fe Railroad .. 183
Austin, John C. 56, 109, 113, 135, 150, 154, 155, 158, 160, 163
Backus, J.J. 97, 106, 155
Ballard Central School 48
Ballin, Hugo 113
Bank of Napa 26, 31
Banks Huntley Building 113
Barham, Guy 135
Barker Brothers 85
Bennett, John 94
Bergstrom Stove & Plow Company 79
Bergstrom, Edwin 79, 87, 91, 94
Berlin, Irving 147
Bern, Arthur 129
Bernhardt, Sarah 87
Bilicke, Albert C. 80, 87
Bilicke-Rowan Fireproof Building Company 80
Biltmore Hotel 87, 146, 158, 183

Biltmore Theater 158
Biscailuz, Eugene W. 181
Blackstone, N.B. 97
Blanchard, M.C. 190
Board of Public Works 147, 154, 157, 158, 159, 160, 161
Bolton 19, 25, 26, 37, 38, 155
Bolton Art Gallery 26
Boone, William E. 37
Boston Block 41
Bovard Administration Building 107
Bovard, George Finley 104, 135, 143
Bowen Park 135
Bowen, Calvin C. 133
Bowen, William M. 106, 130, 133
Bowron, Fletcher 181
Braly Block 13, 74, 77, 79
Braly, John Hyde 74
Breckenfeld, Meta C. 34, 42
Breisch, Kenneth 14, 77, 106
Bridge Hall 107
Briggs, H.B.R. 135
Broadway 17, 55, 59, 62, 64, 67, 70, 115, 146, 150, 163, 173, 187
Bryson Building 55
Budd, Zola 143
Buffalo, New York 92, 110
Bugsy 14, 176
Builder and Contractor 59
Building, Temple Bar 34
Bullard Block 160
Bullock, John G. 165, 173
Bullock's Wilshire 7, 11, 13, 14, 113, 125, 164-179, 192
Bureau of Markets 103
Burton & Parkinson 62
Burton, James Lee 59, 63
Butler Hotel 42
Caliente, Nevada 188
California Arts and Architecture 166
California Bank 116
California Railroad Commission ... 184, 187
California Supreme Court 135, 184, 187
Cambridge 106
Canadian Pacific Railway Company 20

Canterbury 56
Capitain & Krempel 57
Capitain, Frank J. 62
Carr, William 129
Carrick, Frank 93
Caruso, Enrico 87
Cascade School 48
Central Passenger Terminal 187
Chamber of Commerce Building 109
Chandler, Harry 135, 138
Chaplin, Charlie 87
Chaplin, Mildred Harris 87
Charles Mulford Robinson 150
Chavez Ravine 143
Chicago Tribune 155
Chicago White Sox 143
Christie, J.H. 188
City Beautiful movement 150
City Parks Department 147
Civic Center Association 184
Classical Moderne 116
Coe, Sebastian 143
Coliseum 13, 14, 17, 125, 130, 135, 136, 138, 140, 143
Collins, David 166
Colon, Panama 188
Colter, Mary 195
Community Development Association 135, 136, 138
Connecticut Yankees 31
Cook & Hall 158
Covina Junction 98
Crane Company 70
Crocker Bank Building 87
Cromwell, Richard 176
Cryer, George E. 145, 154
Currier Building 56, 62, 63
Currier, A.T. 59
Curtis, Charles 129
Curtlett & Beelman 155, 157, 158
Davies, Marion 176
Day, Benjamin F. 48
Delaney, John 93
Delauney, Sonya 166
DeMille, Cecil B. 146

204

INDEX

Denny, Arthur A. 37
Deverell, William. 55, 200
Dewey, Thomas E. 143
Dietrich, Marlene. 13
Dixon, L.E. 140
Dodgers 143
Doolittle, Jimmy 143
Dorothea, Mary 47
Douglas, Donald W. 120
Dragnet 14
Drake University 133
Duke of Windsor 87
Dunn, Irene 176
DWL Parkinson Architects 125
E.F. Hutton Building 116
Earhart, Amelia 120
Earle, Edwin Tobias 91
Eastman, George L. 147
Edwards, Wildey & Dixon Co 138
Eisenhower, Dwight 143
Eldridge, Arthur 147
Elks Lodge 155
Engel, Edward M. 183
Evening Express 135
Evers, Cecil C. 41
Exposition Building 135
Exposition of Industrial and
    Decorative Arts 169
Exposition Park 104, 135
Fairbanks, Douglas 87
Family Plot 14
Federal Reserve Bank of San Francisco .. 116
Federal Trade Commission 98
Feil & Paradise 173
Field, Scott 77, 125
Fisher, Elmer H. 37
Forest Lawn Memorial Park 119, 122
Formula One World Driver's
    Championship 122
Fort MacArthur 122, 181
Fresno 31, 34, 86
Garbo, Greta 13, 175
Garland, William May 135
Garren, William I. 169
Gaslight 176

General Electric 67
Gerrone, Carlo 161
Gesford, Henry C. 133
Gilman, H.L. 188
Gladding, McBean & Co 195
Goodhue, Bertram Grosvenor 110, 159, 161
Grand Central Market 74, 125
Grauman, Sid 146
Griffith, D.W. 87
Griffith, S.N. 34
Gross, Courtlandt S. 122
Gruenfield, Casper 161
Guaranty Building 92
Gumaer, Adelbert George 110
Gumaer, Florence 110
Hall of Justice 160
Halsey, William F. 143
Hancock Park 173
Hancock, Major Henry 175
Haskell, Fitch 94
Hazard, Henry T. 64
Hearst, William Randolph 176
Heinsbergen, Anthony 161
Henderson, Elmer 143
Henning, W.F. 133
Hill, Helen Naomi 124
Hill, Phil 122
Hines, Thomas S. 14, 170, 181, 200
Hollenbeck Hotel 55
Hollow Fire Clay Blocks 85
Homer Laughlin Building 68, 73, 74, 79, 125
Homer Laughlin China Company 73
Hotel Alexandria 80, 85, 87
Hotel Utah 92, 93
Hughes, Evan 20
Hunt, Myron 77
I. Magnin & Co. 176
Illustrated Daily News 119
Industrial Workers of the World 92
International Motors 124
International Olympic Committee 140
Italian Renaissance 63, 92, 159
Italian Romanesque 104

James Black Masonry and Contracting
    Company 92
Jeffers, William M. 183
Jesuit College and Church 48
Joannes Brothers Company 97
John Paul II 17, 143
Johnson & Hurd 23
Johnson, Lyndon B. 143
Johnson, R.B. 34
Jonathan Club 158
Jones Construction 92
Kansas City Chiefs 143
Kearns Building 92
Kearns, Thomas 91, 92
Kellogg, Fred 135
Kellogg, Pamela Parkinson 63, 109, 113, 122
Kennedy, John F. 17, 143
Kimberly, J. Alfred 79
Kimberly, Nancy E. 79
Kimberly-Clark Corporation 79
King Edward III 87
Kreif, Mayer 166
Lalique 169
Lancashire 14, 19, 26
Lang, Harry 147
Lansbury, Angela 14, 175
Laughlin, Homer 68, 70, 73, 74, 79, 125
LeMaire, Eleanor 173
Lentz, Irene 176
Letts, Arthur 173
Lewis, Carl 143
Lindbergh Airway Beacon 147
Lindbergh, Charles 17, 145
Lion, Henry 161
Liverpool 20, 70
Lockhart, June 175
Lockheed Air Terminal 120
Lockheed Aircraft Corporation 122
Los Angeles Athletic Club 56, 94
Los Angeles Chamber of Commerce .. 183
Los Angeles City Hall 11, 14, 56, 77, 113, 125, 144-163
Los Angeles Daily News 188
Los Angeles Evening Express 79

205

INDEX

Los Angeles Evening Herald and Express 119, 192
Los Angeles Examiner 98, 129, 138, 146, 147, 176, 181, 200
Los Angeles Herald 85, 86, 136
Los Angeles Housing Committee 94
Los Angeles Manual Arts High School 120
Los Angeles Memorial Auditorium 135
Los Angeles Memorial Coliseum 7, 11, 13, 109, 128-143
Los Angeles Municipal Arts Commission 150
Los Angeles Museum of History, Science and Art 135
Los Angeles Produce Exchange 103
Los Angeles Public Library 11, 161
Los Angeles Public Market 97
Los Angeles Public Schools 109
Los Angeles Raiders 143
Los Angeles Rams 143
Los Angeles Stock Exchange 116
Los Angeles Swimming Stadium 140
Los Angeles Telephone Company 73
Los Angeles Times 9, 11, 56, 74, 77, 79, 85, 93, 97, 98, 106, 107, 119, 135, 138, 150, 155, 157, 159, 160, 165, 169, 173, 175, 187, 188, 200
Los Angeles Trust and Savings Bank 99
Los Angeles Union Passenger Terminal 13, 116, 181, 188, 192
Los Angeles Union Terminal Company 97
Los Angeles Wholesale Terminal Market 97, 99
Love In An Elevator 176
Lunden, Samuel 116
M.J. Donahoo Building 34
Mallard, Walter 155
Mantz, Paul 120
Manual Arts High School 104
March Field 99
Mariposa Street 34
Marshall, McClintock 161
Martin, Albert C. 113, 155, 158, 160, 163
Massachusetts Institute of Technology 79, 98, 109

Maximilian Ihmsen 135
McCollister, Melissa 110, 119
McDonald, Angus D. 183
McKim, Mead & White 63
Mechanics Institute of Bolton 20
Mersey 20
Metropolitan Opera House 138
MGM Studios 147
Miami Dolphins 143
Miller, Ray. O. 110
Minneapolis 14, 20, 23
Mitchell, John W. 94, 138
Morgan & Walls 56
Morgan, Octavius 56
Municipal Arts Commission 138, 161
Murder, She Wrote 14, 176
Myers, John S. 157
Napa Collegiate Institute 133
Napa Hills 133
Napa River 34
Napa, California 14, 26, 31, 34, 42, 110, 130, 133
National Football League 143
National Register of Historic Places 179
Navy Lockheed Service Center 122
Neblett, Anne 79
Nebraska State Capitol 159
Neenah, Wisconsin 79
Neutra, Richard 14
Nixon, Patricia 175
O.T. Johnson Building 94
O'Melveny, Henry W. 98, 181
Ochsner, Jeffrey 38
Olson, Culbert 181
Olympic Committee 129, 136
Olympic Games 17, 109, 125, 129, 130, 135, 140, 143
Otis Elevator Company 68
Owens, Jesse 143
Oxford 106
Oxfordshire 56
P.J. Walker Company 170
Pacific Clay Manufacturing Company 85
Pacific Electric Railway 97, 98
Pacific Mutual Insurance Building 120

Pacific School 48
Parade of Nations 129
Park Street Chapel 19
Park View Street 155
Parkinson & Bergstrom 7, 76-95, 120, 135
Parkinson & Evers 41
Parkinson & Parkinson 108-125, 170, 190
Parkinson Archives 77, 125, 200
Parkinson Elevator Company 64
Parkinson Field Associates 125
Parkinson, Austin, and Martin 155, 157, 58, 161
Parkinson, Donald Berthold 62, 109
Parkinson, Donald Wells 115, 122, 124
Parkinson, Florence 119
Parkinson, Powelson, Briney, Bernard & Woodford 124
Parkinson, Thomas 19
Pasadena Civic Auditorium 94
Patton, George S. 17
Paul Mantz Air Services 120
Pearl Harbor 14
Pentagon, the 94
Peters, Jock D. 166, 173
Philips Academy 79
Phinney, Guy C. 42
Pickford, Mary 87
Picture of Dorian Gray, The 176
Pierson, Wallace 119
Pink Floyd 17, 143
Pitkin, C.S. 70
Plummer, John C. 175
Pomona College 143
porte cochere 13, 170
Putnam & Valentine 86
Raleigh and Harmon 92
Reagan, Ronald 143
Reeves, Claude 106
Richardson, Henry Hobson 37
Riviera Country Club 140
Roberts, John 19, 20
Rogers, Ginger 176
Rolling Stones 17, 143
Romanesque 47, 159
Rooney, Dr. C.E. 116

206

INDEX

Roosevelt, Franklin D. 17, 143
Roosevelt, Theodore. 87
Rose Bowl. 140
Rosslyn Hotel 94
Rough Magic 176
Rowan Building 87
Rowan, Robert A. 80
Rush, Jud R. 98
Sachs, Herman. 113, 161, 166, 170, 195
Salt Lake City 91, 92
Salt Lake Railroad 109
Salt Lake Tribune 92
San Diego Ship Building Company 99
Santa Fe Railroad 55, 97, 183, 188
Santa Monica. 109, 110, 116, 119, 122, 124, 173, 190, 208
Schenck, Joseph 146
Schiaparelli, Elsa 169
Schindler, Pauline G. 166
Schindler, Rudolph 14
Schultze and Weaver 158
Seattle 7, 14, 34, 36-53, 56-57, 59, 63, 92, 104, 110, 129, 200
Seattle Athletic Club 48
Seattle National Bank 47
Seattle Pacific University 48
Security Building 87, 94
Shaw, Frank L. 190
Sheffield Scientific School 79
Sheridan 86
Shoup, Paul. 97
Snafel & Prawn 34
Snyder, Meredith P. 135
South Seattle School 48
Southern California Savings Bank ... 74, 77
Southern California Telephone Company Building 116
Southern Pacific Central Station. 184
Southern Pacific Railroad 55, 97, 183, 187, 188, 190
Southwest Builder and Contractor, The 195
Southwestern Law School 125, 179
Spanish Colonial Revival 109
Spanish Mission 188

Spanish Provincial 195
Spanish Renaissance 80
Sparks, R. S. 160
Speed of Transportation mural 170
Sprague Electric Company 67
Sprague, Frank J. 67
Spreckels Building 115
Spring Street 17, 56, 85, 86, 90, 113, 116, 150
Springsteen, Bruce 17
Squire Block. 38
St. Augustine-by-the Sea Church 119
St. James Episcopal Church 110
St. Luke's Day School 19
Stadium, Harvard 138
Star Trek: First Contact 14
Starr, Kevin 17, 55, 130, 165, 192, 200
Stephens, Jess E. 157, 187
Stewart, Anita 87
Stillwell, Joseph 143
Stojana, Gjura 166
Story, Walter P. 145
Stowell Block 56, 59
Stowell, Thomas B. 106
Strasbourg Cathedral 11, 119
Streamline 116, 120, 192
Subway Terminal Building 158
Sullivan, Louis. 92
Super Bowl 17, 143
Swinton 19
Taft, William Howard 87, 93
Taj Mahal 11, 119
Telegraph Hill 26
Title Guarantee Building 113
Title Insurance and Trust Company 113
Tolan, Eddie. 130
Trent, Goodwin M. 115
Union Oil Building 94
Union Pacific 183, 187, 188, 190
Union Station 7, 11, 13, 14, 109, 116, 125, 180-195
United Artists 87
University of Southern California (USC) 11, 13, 14, 17, 104, 107, 122-125, 133, 135, 143, 190

University of Southern California Methodist Church 133
USC Trojans 17, 125
Utah State Bank 93
Valentino, Rudolph 87
Van Nuys Hotel 57
Von KleinSmid, Rufus Bernhard 107
Wagner, Dr. F.J. 110
Walls, John A. 56
Walter, Edgar 116
War of the Worlds 14
Washington Hotel 92
Washington Magazine 37
Washington Redskins 143
Wayne, John 13, 175
Wells, Frances Grace 109
Wells, Ralph Evans 109
Western Union 99
Westlake, H. W. 64, 147
Whittlesey, Austin 161
Wholesale Terminal Branch 99
Wholesale Terminal Market 97, 98, 103, 104
Willkie, Wendell L. 143
Wilson, Fred 93
Wilson, Woodrow 87, 107
Winnett, Percy 169
Wirth, R.J. 188
Woodacres 124
Woodford & Bernard 124, 125
Woodford, Parkinson, Wynn & Partners 125
Woollett, William Lee 94
Workman, Boyle 155
World War II 143
Worthington Pump & Machinery Corporation 67
Wright, Frank Lloyd 14, 74, 158, 166
Wright, Lloyd 158
Yale University 79
Young, Robert Brown 57
Young, Clement C. 161

612:—NEW CITY HALL, LOS ANGELES, CALIF.

LOS ANGELES CITY HALL; POSTCARD

Iconic Vision: John Parkinson, Architect of Los Angeles

By Stephen Gee

Copyright© 2013 Stephen Gee

Design by Lentini Design, Los Angeles

10 9 8 7 6 5 4 3 2 1

ISBN-13 978-1-62640-008-5

All rights reserved.
No part of this book may be reproduced or transmitted in any form or by any means, electronic or mechanical, including photocopying, recording, or by an information storage and retrieval system, without express written permission from the publisher. Printed in Canada.

Names and trademarks of products are the property of their registered owners.

Library of Congress Cataloging-in-Publication Data is available

ANGEL CITY PRESS

Published by Angel City Press
2118 Wilshire Boulevard, Number 880
Santa Monica, California 90403
+1.310.395.9982
www.angelcitypress.com